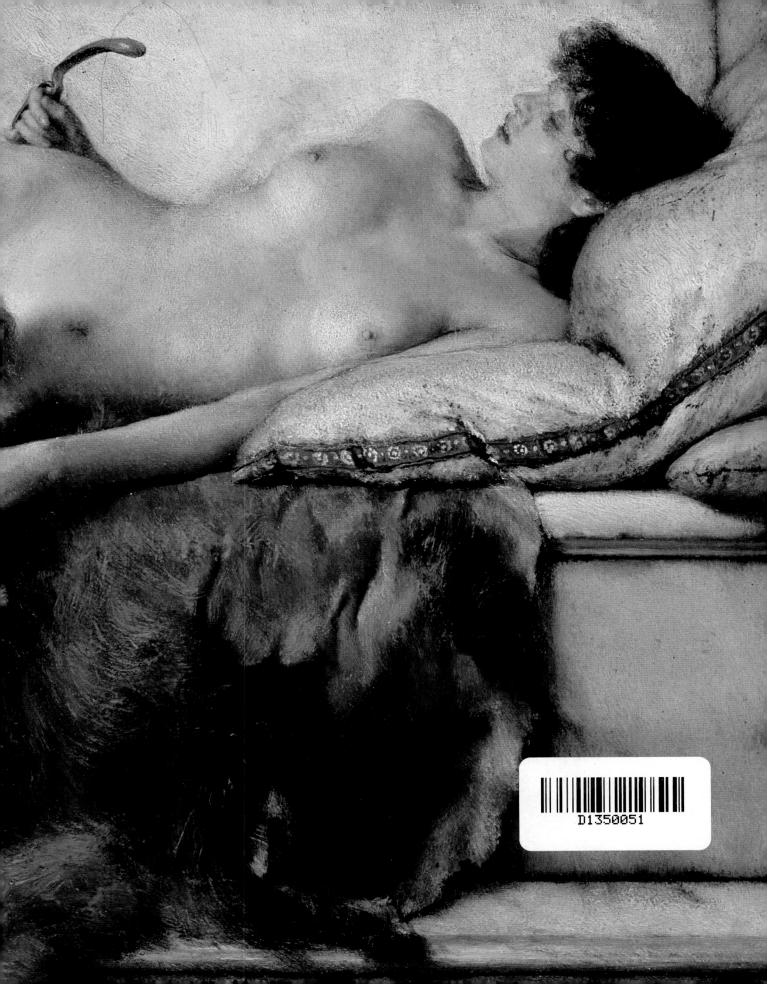

Dangerous Women

Thanks to Cyril Lécosse, Florence Colombani,
Marion Doublet, Marie-Catherine Audet

Translated from the French by
David Radzinowicz

Design
Dune Lunel

Copyediting
Penelope Isaac

Typesetting
Anne Lou Bissières

Proofreading
Helen Woodhall

Color Separation
Couleurs d'image

Printed in Slovenia by Krater

Distributed in North America by Rizzoli
International Publications, Inc.

This book is part of a series originally conceived of
and designed by Elisabeth Sandmann Verlag, Munich.

Simultaneously published in French as
Les femmes qui aiment sont dangereuses
© Flammarion, S. A., Paris, 2009

English-language edition
© Flammarion, S. A., Paris, 2009

87, quai Panhard et Levassor
75647 Paris Cedex 13

editions.flammarion.com

10 11 12   3 2 1

ISBN-13: 978-2-08-030128-4

Dépôt légal: 01/2010

p. 2–3: *The Tepidarium*, Sir Lawrence Alma-Tameda,
oil on panel, 9 ½ x 13 in. (24 x 33 cm), Lady Lever Art
Gallery, National Museums Liverpool
p. 8–9: *Laus Veneris*, Edward Burne-Jones, 1873–75,
oil on canvas, 48 x 72 in. (122 x 183 cm), Tyne & Wear
Museums, Newcastle
p. 158–59: *Le Verrou* (*The Bolt*), Jean-Honoré Fragonard,
c. 1778, oil on canvas, 28 x 36 in. (73 x 93 cm),
Musée du Louvre, Paris

Laure Adler and Élisa Lécosse

Dangerous Women

The Perils of Muses and Femmes Fatales

Flammarion

Contents

12
Between Rapture
and Ecstasy
Women in love know who
they are and where they are going
Laure Adler

34
Woman and Love:
Models, myths,
and fables

66
Seductress
and Enchantress

90
Emancipation
and Transgression
in Love

116
Women
and Power

138
The "Eternal
Feminine"
Muses, victims,
and femmes fatales

Laure Adler
Between Rapture and Ecstasy
Women in love know
who they are and
where they are going

"After being alive, the next hardest work is having sex."

Andy Warhol

"You're killing me, you're doing me good." This litany, from a French woman to her Japanese lover, is from Marguerite Duras's script for the Alain Resnais film, *Hiroshima mon amour*; it resounds like the oncoming violence of the desire that seizes women when they fall in love. And so they fall. There is the feeling of dropping, but also—to remain in Duras's universe (someone who, in the twentieth century, has best written of women in love)—a sense of abduction, rapture, voiding of the self.

So what happens when Cupid's dart hits a woman? For centuries, everything carried on as if women had no rights. Love could be none of her business. This was what men had decided: ecclesiastics, aristocrats, hygienists, pseudo-specialists in female moods, etc.

Still, when struck by misfortune, women had the right to weep—composing innumerable figures of the Mater Dolorosa—or to prepare themselves for an angel bringing glad tidings: finally, in the whole history of humanity, a woman had been appointed to give birth to the child of God without having to be penetrated.

It is hard to avoid the woman who illuminates all with her beauty, her transparency, the perfect oval of her face, the depth of her gaze, a woman in love, painted, overpainted, overdepicted; the woman who has for all time preoccupied the desire of painters, commissioned or not: the Virgin Mary.

Out in the world, she pursues you: through museums and churches, in public spaces, at the crossroads of the most deserted paths. She protects us, reassures us, gazes at us, often as if she wanted to upbraid us, as if she wanted to tell us: I was not in love, to be in love was a state I was unaware of, so why was I selected to conceive within my body something that, by definition, should remain the invisible, the insurmountable, the very essence of the divine?

The Annunciation, **Ambrogio Lorenzetti,** 1344,
wood panel, 51 x 59 in. (130 x 150 cm), Pinacoteca Nazionale, Siena

VIRGINS ARE NOT WHAT PEOPLE TRIED TO MAKE US BELIEVE THEY WERE

The figure of the Virgin has lost nothing of its fascination. The shock waves of the amorous magnetism that grabs one round the throat when one looks at her continues to have an effect on the image we have of women in love, from the Ancien Régime to the modern era.

Far from being passive, ecstatically awaiting an event that is by definition unthinkable, the Virgin can seem astonished and not necessarily overjoyed when she is told what is a senseless piece of news—senseless in that it is not destined to throw her sensuality into panic: the fact that she is to be touched by Grace without having to enjoy it bodily. This is clear, for instance, in a picture by Lorenzo Lotto, *The Annunciation* of Recalcati, dated 1527, in which she is seen in a startled attitude, with the angel placed behind her, and, in the center, a black cat, an omen of the bad news—of the misfortune, even—that is about to descend upon her.

So she is a virgin, certainly, but she is not so happy to be and to stay one. A wise virgin in the sense that she knows she must be welcoming without inseminating; a virgin who conveys great tidings that concern her only in her stunned astonishment; a virgin vessel, anxious to understand the angel's message, as indicated by Gabriel's pose in Ambrogio Lorenzetti's *Annunciation* of

1314, where the archangel's thumb is turned over backwards: behind him the mystery, in front of him the Virgin—how can he play the intercessor so that Mary can become the handmaid of the Lord? How can one touch the untouchable?

A sexualized virgin too: in his *Annunciation* in London, Filippo Lippi turns her into a bride. Her head already bears a halo and she is glancing down at the Book of Books; but her dress displays a hole. Level with the navel, a buttonhole without a button opens up for the supernatural impact of the beam emitted by the dove. A virgin transpierced by love! Specialists in the history of painting, such as Samuel Y. Edgerton, propose erudite interpretations based on the use of optics in medieval theology. I, however, prefer

the analysis given by Daniel Arrasse in *Le Détail*,[1]
his great book subtitled "A History of Painting in
Close-up." As he sees it, this hole marks a secret,
not so much of the mystery of the Incarnation,
but as evidence of the painter's veneration for the
female body, even the Virgin's, in the way of all
those erotic metaphors in the Song of Songs. For
instance when the lover says to the Sulamite: "The
joints of thy thighs are like jewels, the work of the
hands of a cunning workman. Thy navel is like a
round goblet, which wanteth not liquor: thy belly
is like a heap of wheat set about with lilies."

Is it really such a coincidence that, eight years
later, in Prato, at the time of the festival of the
Virgin Mary, Filippo Lippi was to abduct (with the
girl's consent, let it be said), a young nun, Lucrezia

Buti, who, while still in the convent, had sat for him
for a picture of the Virgin that he was preparing for
an altarpiece?

The history of painting presents many such
examples of painters capturing for all eternity
the faces and bodies of women who embody
mythological and religious figures, and then entering
into relationships centered on appropriation,
possession, eroticization.

LOVE'S DARTS

Eros deifies, and we, who look at these pictures
as if time has been suspended, also enter into a
relation of vertiginous love, as Rainer Maria Rilke
expresses so well in his *Testament*. He gazes on a
reproduction of Van Eyck's *Lucca Madonna*: she is
depicted totally absorbed in the physical contact
with her child, whom she suckles next to a window
ledge on which stand two apples. Rilke writes:
"And suddenly I desired, I desired, oh, I desired
with all the fervor of which my heart has ever been
capable, I desired, not to be one of the little apples
in the picture, not one of those painted apples on
the painted window ledge—even that seemed to
me too high a destiny—no: to become the soft,
the negligible, the imperceptible shadow of one of
these apples—such was the desire into which my
entire being was gathered."[2]

Instantaneousness of desire. Presence of an
existence. Phantoms of the past. Why do all these

The Virgin of Lucca, Jan Van Eyck, 1435–40,
oil on panel, 26 x 19 ½ in. (65.5 x 49.5 cm),
Städelsches Kunstinstitut und Städtische Galerie, Frankfurt-am-Main

women depicted as the Virgin in our museums seem to be here, in this world, in our world, since we can plunge our eyes into theirs, we can admire the beauty of their face, the perfection of their body, down to the most intimate details, reveling in the pleasure their aptitude for ecstasy affords them, their sense of abandonment, the sensual attraction that their sometimes lascivious poses exert?

CAN WOMEN BE IN LOVE WITH THEMSELVES?

Sculpture as well as painting possesses a strange ability to project into our imagination the spiritual, the bodily experiences of the cohorts of women who remind us of the elevated status they enjoyed in the most ancient civilizations. I find proof in a stone carving entitled *The Venus of Laussel*, dating to 25,000-20,000 BCE, or the drawing of a figurine from Malta, between 4000 and 3000 BCE, recto-verso, called the *Masturbating Woman*: the front shows the woman lifting her left arm towards the back of the head while her other hand caresses her genitals; her feet are pointing and bent backward—a sign of a supreme state of pleasure?—the breasts are heavy, the navel pronounced; but the head has not been drawn. The verso shows the back scored vertically, with the arm and feet in the same position.

This ability to dissociate sexual pleasure from reproduction, this aptitude for pleasuring oneself,

this practice of seminal secretion reminds us that women are not mere receptacles that only sperm can warm and so justify their existence; that make them mothers and mothers only, the only reason they have the right to or the possibility of making love. It also reminds us that a woman's body does not only secrete blood, a sign of weakness, a proof of defeat, of sterile sexual intercourse, but also a froth, the milk of pleasure, analogous to male semen.

Women searching for the acme of pleasure are "wet," as the prevailing sexual parlance has it. They get wet for themselves when, controlling their body, they make it into an instrument of their own pleasure, perfectly attuned to their ability for self-pleasuring.

It's hard not to think here of Catherine Millet's book *The Sexual Life of Catherine M.*, in which the female narrator evokes all her acts with a naturalness that can only be admired, drawing the following philosophical lesson: "Talking about pleasure, extreme pleasure, is much more a work of art. Anyway, isn't it commonly compared to being transported out of oneself and the world, and therefore outside time as well? And is there the added, aporetic problem of wanting to identify and recognize something that no one has yet described to you, or only sketchily."[3]

Catherine Millet is right: girls are told nothing, or as good as nothing, about sexual pleasure, and in a new text that accompanies the mass-market

edition of her book entitled "Why and how," she states specifically that she intends her book for women. Her style is hyperrealist: she slices up her surroundings as if framing a shot, showing us, in the manner of a photograph, all there is to see, to feel, in such-or-such a position—with or without a companion in pleasure. The latter are figures, necessary components in setting up the erotic game and for attaining greater intensity, rather than individuals with their own excitements, feelings, passions. It little matters who they are, what they might want, or if they will be seen again.

The absence of any bond is part of a conspiracy hatched for pleasure, for her pleasure, for her inner notion of pleasure, as she ascends toward an interiorization of herself, the construction of her identity, her most secret recomposition, her desire to form a single body with herself, and—if just for a moment—to rest awhile.

It is not hunger for sex that spurs Catherine M. to scamper from orgy to orgy, but a secret instinct that makes her dream that there, precisely in places where she is not recognized, where in others' eyes she is no longer herself, she will get to know a little more (about) who she is, how far she can go in her capacity for unfolding her body to forestall dissemination, to dislocate herself less, to achieve her own center of gravity.

Her writing is entirely predicated on her passion for painting and the text can be read as a series of pictures. The drive to see is pushed to its paroxysm. What is seeing? What is it to be seen? What is the meaning of being seen making love while seeing others perform the same act?

Because, if one can speak about sexuality, about sexual intercourse being interchanged and repeated in ceremonies determined by the theatrical, it is not impossible that there, in this duly ring-fenced preserve of the duty of sex, the only, the painful point is, again, love—mad love, pure love, love on occasion for oneself. One does not go to an orgy in the way one goes shopping in the supermarket. One does not enter an apartment masked, disguised, scented, dressed in underclothing specially selected to operate well in various sexual strategies, as one would enter a sex shop to glimpse a snippet from a porn video or handle a whip or two. It requires far more courage and determination to face one's adversaries, who will become—for a brief flash—allies, who, on the

Woman masturbating, drawing after a figure from Malta, c. 4000-3000 BCE

battlefield of desire, have as much to gain in the fleetingness of pleasure as to lose in the melancholy at the end of the game and in the hopelessness that follows.

This authorization that women give themselves before stalking those minefields of sex and love so long proscribed them is manifested in the entire oeuvre of Louise Bourgeois, an artist long neglected but who today is considered an international contemporary art icon. Why, though, did she have to reach the category of "old lady" to be seen, to be recognized? Was what she had to show us so explosive that she had to attain a venerable age before her work could become "visible"? I cannot help recalling a remark of Françoise Héritier's *Masculin/Féminin 1*[4] on the peculiar status of menopausal women; an awkward, taboo subject, skirted over in the history of the relations between the genders, though it demonstrates how the individual status of women tends to alter—for the better—from the time they can no longer produce children. They become more powerful in character, in moral strength, in authority. In short, they are considered more highly than when they were better able to seduce and capture men.

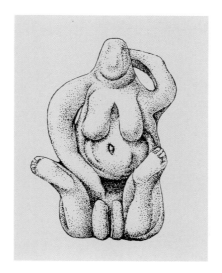

WOMEN WITH HEARTS OF MEN

Women described as having the "heart of a man" live in Canada: certain Native American women of the Piegan tribe (described by Lewis Oscar in 1941) behave in a particular manner that is entirely accepted in an otherwise perfectly patriarchal society. The Piegan feminine ideal is still shaped by gentleness, tenderness, and humility. But a few of the eldest intervene in public life like the men and even attend their ceremonies. Better still: they perform their allotted tasks more effectively than the menfolk—including their husbands—and have the right to prohibit them from undertaking certain actions because they know a priori that the men are not as effective as they are. Moreover, even though they might be old and, generally, already married several times, the society in which they live still thinks of them as sexually active and unconventional in their love lives. In the same manner as men, these women have the right to organize sun dances and participate in trials by ordeal. As Francoise Héritier puts it, they have the "force."

Self-portrait, **Louise Bourgeois,** 1942,
ink on paper, 11 x 8 ½ in. (27.9 x 21.5 cm), Musée national d'art moderne-Centre Georges Pompidou

Women in love are dangerous because the power of their desire can disturb the so-called natural imbalance that has existed between the sexes since the dawn of humanity; sometimes one feels they might be able to reconfigure it, turn it upside down even.

A woman in love is worth a hundred. By her sexual power and her knowledge of things of the heart, she can, in giving herself to the one she has chosen, entrap him in the snare of her desire and make him her equal or even her slave. In every latitude, female desire has always been perceived of as stronger, more bewitching, more mysterious than male desire. Louise Bourgeois can be placed in this category of women with the "heart of a man." She makes this very point when stating of her work: "It is not an image I am after; it is not an idea. It is an emotion that I want to recreate; an emotion of desire; a gift, and an idea of destruction."[5]

After thirty years of neglect, Louise Bourgeois is now much in the media spotlight and her daring as an artist is acknowledged. Even before the emergence of feminism, this ardent militant was already tackling subjects both significant and proscribed to women—in both historical and political terms: the body and the organic, the transsexual and the sexual. Bourgeois stood these on their head, bestowing on herself characteristics she cheekily purloined from men: think of her *Self-Portrait*, dated 1942, where the lower half of the face as well as part of the neck is covered with a beard.

Marie-Laure Bernadac, in a thorough examination of this piece, classifies it among what she dubs "original images."[6] Bourgeois painted herself in this manner while still a young woman (she was thirty-three at the time), with the features of an ageless androgyne who has succeeded, through art, in transcending sex and time: an eternalized Louise Bourgeois.

ARE WOMEN IN LOVE REALLY WOMEN LIKE THE OTHERS?

In many societies, women are not regarded as legal persons and exceptional conditions need to be fulfilled before they are—temporarily—deemed as such. Though then they cannot remain women, but have to be transformed into men-women, as Françoise Héritier demonstrates in *Masculin/Féminin II*. It is when the city is in mortal danger that women are authorized to fight in the place of male soldiers and, thus, to attain the status of men: in Argos, for example, they were, on occasion, permitted to sport a false beard.... Society can then admit—in the sense of "allow" rather than "recognize"—"the possible presence of a virile heart in a woman's body that makes her an exceptional being."[7] Françoise Héritier's words can equally be applied to the artistic career, the tireless risk-taking, and the reflection on sexual difference that characterizes Louise Bourgeois's oeuvre.

Regarding the various periods of an output that combine introspection with a quest for theoretical abstraction, Louise Bourgeois's position seems to echo the mental constructs of certain so-called primitive societies, turning herself, as it were, into a shaman: hence her series of drawings on bones, the skeleton, the spinal column—the load-bearing components of the human body.

Perhaps her perspective on male/female relationships has links with ancient beliefs—found in both the Sumerian and the Egyptian civilization— of how seed is stored in bones? The Sumerians believed that living beings were produced by the seeds of their ancestors and that these germs

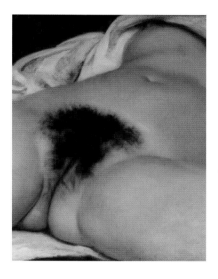

were destroyed when their ancestors disappeared. Hence the importance of preserving bones, to ensure at once the survival of the ancestors in the other world and the bond between the living and the dead. In Ancient Egypt, the seed, source of all life, was also contained in bones. It was thought to collect in the spinal column, flowing from there into the neighboring phallus. Specialists such as Jean Yoyote have studied these questions. In any case, such beliefs can even persist down to the present day. In present-day Egypt, for example, men who have had too much sex say they have backache, that their semen has been completely sucked out of their bones.

What happens to a woman's body when it is sexually overworked? It's not her back that suffers, but her genitals. This we know thanks to statements by nineteenth- and twentieth-century prostitutes in Paris, locked up in brothels or working the grand boulevards: in police interrogations preserved at the Arsenal Library, they speak of their sexual organs being sore due to the constant repetition of the act. They also frequently talk, not so much of society's scorn for their condition or of the violence they suffer, as of their joy when they

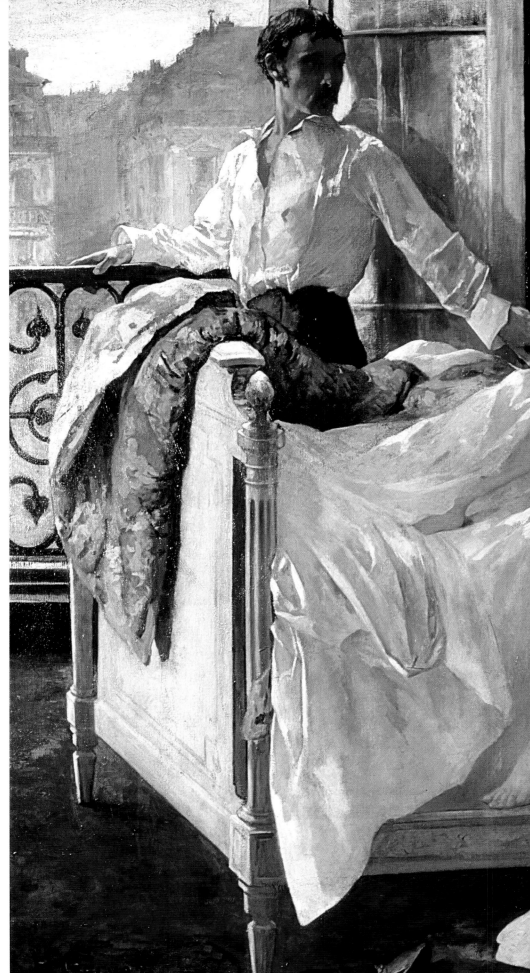

La Rolla, **Henri Gervex,** 1878,
oil on canvas, 69 x 86 ½ in. (175 x 220 cm),
Musée des Beaux-Arts, Bordeaux

become mothers, when they first see their child, when they know that it will be protected so that one day—once they reach an age that allows them to become women; that is, women without sex—they will be able to see it again.

WITH WHOM AND WITH WHAT ARE WOMEN IN LOVE?

The ambivalence between the mother and the whore is one of the most widespread, most obsessive old saws commonly believed of a woman in love, whatever her age, her condition, or the continent in which she lives. Too much sex undermines the idea many men have of a woman, wanting her solely to be a sex object; always provided she is not human in any true sense, but a series of orifices. In a series of works on the penis, Louise Bourgeois illustrates this age-old notion, taking it up the better to denounce it. She has also written of a fundamental experience of her vision of the relations between men and women she had when an adolescent. Her father took her to a New York nightclub: on leaving, they came across some prostitutes in the street. "Well, let's see the girls," he suggests. He has the girls parade up and down in front of him, one after the other. While his daughter looks on, they take up poses in an effort to be attractive to him. Louise sees her father looking at them in turn, one after the other, until his eyes begin to shine lustfully. A traumatic,

crucial scene. Bourgeois recalls: "I identified with those that failed. It's about defining my low self-esteem. You realize how terribly difficult it is to make it. The desire to please is the motivation and there are no rules. It's Russian roulette."[8]

Woman cannot be reduced to a slit that a penis is meant to fill. A woman also has hips, breasts. She is Gaia, a mother goddess, a uterine power. And what if, by way of her sexual attributes, she possesses the erotic potential of being able to put herself on an equal footing with men when in love? Yes, a woman can desire a male sex; yes, a woman can stroke a male sex; yes, a woman can, in taking care of that male sex, comfort him ... for being just a man!

The work entitled *Fillette*, dated 1968, and made famous in a photograph by Robert Mappelthorpe, is a hanging sculpture made out of latex—a male member that can be taken for a newborn. It is soft, tender, and, approaching it, one can experience the same excitement a mother feels when sniffing the scent of a little child or, when cradling it against her, as if trying to pull it back into her body. Thus, a penis is a nice thing. One just has to know how to tame it and to learn how to make use of it.

As Louise Bourgeois confirmed by being photographed with her child-phallus: "When I carry a little phallus like that in my arms, well, it seems like a nice little object, it's certainly not an object I would wish to harm, that's clear. The niceness is directed toward men."[9]

It is hard here not to sense the artist's humor, her flair for provocation, for sexual transgression; as if, with age, she had managed to literally incorporate the male dimension of sexual power that all women harbor without necessarily being aware of.

Did Louise Bourgeois ultimately become a woman with the "heart of a man"? In any case, in a series of suspended works like *Janus*, double phalli that revolve on their axis, she will certainly introduce the masculine into the feminine, visualizing at the same time the slit and the phallus, presenting us with a vision of a world in which man and woman, in the act of love, interlock to form a single body, erotized in the extreme and no longer a Love Object but a Love Subject, finally at peace with the Other, in harmony with oneself.

HOW CAN ONE TELL WHEN A WOMAN IS IN LOVE?

A woman can be aroused, of course, but it is not very visible. When a man has an erection it is clear for all to see. A woman getting wet can, if she so wishes, continue to become wetter and wetter without anyone noticing. The power of female sexual love remains concealed. It is a surge that can break over us, but we don't have to make it visible. "*The Ravishing*," writes Marguerite Duras for *Lol V. Stein*—who is literally abducted by sexual pleasure; not when she makes love, but when she spots, ten years after being jilted, the girlfriend with whom she then was making love in a hotel that she knew at the time of her engagement. She wants to see, or rather she wants to get up close, without being seen; stretched out in the rye field, invisible to the others. She is aware of what is happening and the excitation even reaches back to the idea that it is happening not *for* her, but in her. A woman does not inevitably require a man to be pleasured. In fact, there she is, shattered, tired of being herself, watchful; then in that slow release, that wonderful feebleness, as the author writes, that reaches suffocation point: "The rye rustles beneath her loins. Young, early summer rye. Her eyes riveted on the lighted window, a woman harkens to the void—feeding upon, devouring this nonexistent, invisible spectacle, the light from a room where others are."[10]

Teresa of Ávila, **Francisco Goya (attributed),** nineteenth century, oil on canvas, 53 ½ x 38 ½ in. (136 x 98 cm), Château de Villandry

What is happening? Jacques Lacan points out that in this instant she is present to herself, but that, since childhood, she had been *next to* herself. This capturing of the self by the self, this ravishment, has links with mystic ecstasy. In effect, when one rereads St. Teresa of Ávila's autobiography and interprets her observations in the light of erotic desire (as Julia Kristeva does so brilliantly in her book[11]), one discovers that hidden, secret, torrential power she possesses of being able to take pleasure in herself by thinking of and contemplating her love of God.

It is hardly a coincidence that philosophers hold the opinion that only female mystics have access to truth. Probably because with them the conspicuous in sex remains buried and their approach to the truth is direct, unmediated: it is God who speaks in Teresa, a receptacle for his Word. Teresa becomes a body permeated by this union: she is ravished—that's what she writes. Slave of love, she adds. She deals with God as an equal. She needs nothing, nobody, except for a few books, such as St. Augustine's *Confessions*, and solitude. Teresa evokes moments of genuinely delicious pleasure, of deflection from the source, of that sovereign process "of being filled up from all sides." She says she was "engulfed into Him."

Women mystics often become anorexic, as if the material body formed a barrier to union. The mystical body then yields to the voluntary oblivion of the physical; then it is confined to a soul tensed in the desire for union with the inexpressible.

In the history of Western thought, this constitutes one of the rare exceptions in which the body is no longer seen as dominating the mind of woman. Because, in general, if ever the mind gains the upper hand, then woman is as good as lost to love.

So woman is allowed beauty and allotted a role as a muse, as seductive inveigler, as inspiration. As Kant puts it: "Laborious learning or painful pondering, even if a woman should greatly succeed in it, destroy the merits that are proper to her sex, and because of their rarity they can make of her an object of admiration; but at the same time, they will weaken the charms with which she exercises her great power over the opposite sex."[12]

Woman is what she lets others see of herself. If she uses her mind, as Geneviève Fraisse mischievously points out in *La Différence des sexes*,[13] it means forfeiting her body. In

The Turkish Bath, **Jean Auguste Dominique Ingres,** 1862,
oil on canvas on wood, 42 ½ x 43 ⅓ in. (108 x 110 cm), Musée du Louvre, Paris

consequence, one understands why so few women have risked doing so. And yet, women are less and less concerned with their appearance and increasingly seek to exercise the mind. Beauty and intelligence are apportioned much less systematically than our philosophers—be their names Nietzsche, Schopenhauer, or Kant—give credit for. Yes, men can be stupid and ugly and women intelligent and beautiful. Yes, women can have other desires than the one assigned them by Rousseau: "to be versed in the knowledge of men."[14] For they are rich in their own vein of knowledge; knowledge of love that opens the door to the supreme desire: access to truth.

Because truth is woman, and it has to be laid bare in order to know it.

IF YOU WANT TO KNOW MORE ABOUT LOVE, ASK WOMEN

Today, luckily, the eternal feminine is no more. The genders are becoming less and less distinguishable; there is more and more dialectic between the feminine and the masculine; an erotic, ebullient homosexuality, lived as a culture, a vision of the world, and a new way of conceiving pleasures of love, increasingly asserts itself.

Today, alas, non-normative sexual behavior— i.e., which does not allow for the reproduction of the species—is still rejected by a majority of the population. Sometimes such disapproval can even degenerate into acts of violence against those (of both genders) whose sexual "model" differs from theirs. Today, in the artistic, conceptual, philosophical, and literary fields, the very concept of sex is being shattered and fragmented into myriad meanings, freed from all constraint, spawning new ways of thinking expressed in new forms of morphing, role-swapping, and overlap between the sexes.

Are we witnessing the birth of a third sex? New medical technologies allow homosexual women to be made pregnant; a man, born male, can be turned into a woman—but intolerance is growing against this new, transsexual world. One chooses to be other than what one is. Anatomy is no longer our destiny. Biological gender does not always square with sexual identity. The male sex yields its prerogatives; certain men are not afraid to proclaim their feminine side. The female sex, without shame, claims her share at the banquet of sexual pleasure. This sex, for so long the receptacle of the pleasure of the other, demands to be autonomous and to procure its own pleasure, alone. Catherine Millet again: "For a large part of my life I fucked without regard to pleasure. First I should concede that for someone who has known so many partners, no outcome was ever so guaranteed as when I sought it alone. I control the pitch of my pleasure to the nearest fraction of a second, which isn't possible when you have to take into account someone else and when you depend

Amnesia (detail from the diptych), **Sophie Calle**, 1992,
black-and-white photograph, aluminum frames (x2) 67 x 39 ⅓ and 19 ½ x 19 ½ in.
(170 x 100 cm and 50 x 50 cm), 1/5 F (#6689)

No matter how hard I try, I never remember the color of a man's eyes or
the shape and size of his sex. But I decided a wife should know these things.
So I made an effort to fight this amnesia. I now know he has green eyes.

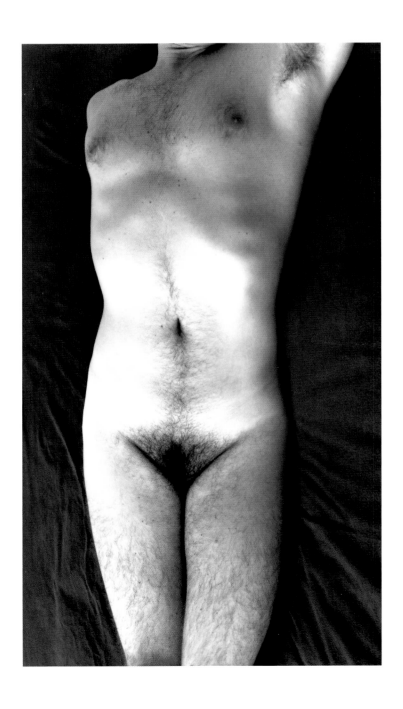

Portrait of the Lovers, **Annette Messager**, 1977,
80 x 111 in. (204 x 282 cm), FRAC Aquitaine (purchase from the Gillepsie-Laage-Salomon Gallery, Paris)

on their moves and not on your own."[15] Catherine M. thus claims to masturbate with the punctuality of a functionary. Is it sheer coincidence that, as a professional art critic, Catherine Millet's trade is looking? Or that her first erotic shivers took place in a painter's studio? Is it just chance that this love for painting is fueled by an intellectually highly structured libidinal economy?

How is one meant to take the following definition of painting by the Goncourt Brothers:

"We have virtually replaced woman, in other words the pretext for love … by pictures. For us, everything not conveyed through art resembles raw meat"?

This journey through the history of art invites us to examine for ourselves the various metamorphoses of woman in love as depicted by women and men alike. All, without exception, come up against that best-kept, most opaque secret in the world: how can one imprison, forever, for oneself, the vertigo caused by love?

1 Daniel Arrasse. *Le Détail, pour une histoire rapprochée de la peinture.* Paris: Flammarion, 1992, 2008 / **2** Rainer Maria Rilke. *Testament.* Paris: Seuil, 1983. / **3** Catherine Millet. *The Sexual Life of Catherine M.* (tr. A. Hunter). London: Serpent's Tail, 2002, p. 177. / **4** Françoise Héritier. *Masculin/Féminin, vol. 1, La pensée de la différence.* Paris: Odile Jacob, 1995. / **5** Christiane Meyer Thoss. *Louise Bourgeois, Designing for free fall.* London: Art Data, 1992. / **6** Marie-Laure Bernadac. *Louise Bourgeois.* Paris: Flammarion, 2006. / **7** Françoise Héritier, *Masculin/ Féminin, vol. 2, Dissoudre la hiérarchie,* Paris: Odile Jacob, 2002. / **8** Bernadac, *Louise Bourgeois,* p. 178. / **9** Bernadac, *Louise Bourgeois,* p. 107. / **10** Marguerite Duras. *The Ravishing of Lol Stein* (tr. R. Seaver). New York: Pantheon, 1964, p. 54 / **11** Julia Kristeva. *Thérèse mon amour.* Paris: Fayard, 2008. / **12** I. Kant. *Observations on the Feeling of the Beautiful and the Sublime* (tr. J. T. Goldthwait). Berkeley, LA: University of California Press, 1960, p. 78 [1764]. / **13** Geneviève Fraisse. *La différence des sexes.* Paris: PUF, 1996. / **14** Rousseau. *Pensées.* Paris: Seuil, 1984. / **15** Millet, *The Sexual Life of Catherine M.,* p. 199.

Woman and Love: Models, myths, and fables

From primitive societies, supposedly free of sexual discrimination, through the burden of the Judeo-Christian tradition, up to contemporary art, the representation of women in love tells the story of the relationship of men and women, and of artists and viewers, to the female body.

In the collective imagination, as well as in Western art, womankind occupies two poles of the sacred, malevolent power as well as fecundity and bounty. Because she gives life, she has exerted a mysterious fascination, which may have materialized in prehistoric times in the cult of the "mother goddess" or "great goddess." Primitive religions abound in diverse incarnations of this "sacred feminine." It is manifest in various figures in the ancient Sumerian, Greek, Roman, Celtic, Scandinavian, and Hindu religions. In polytheistic Greece, she takes the form of cults dedicated to Isis, Cybele, Demeter, Gaia, and Aphrodite, all generally associated with the Earth as provider. This fascination for woman persists, under a different guise, in the Judeo-Christian tradition.

As an object of veneration or mistrust, the feminine symbolizes antagonistic principles: the benevolence, love, and purity of the Virgin Mary are opposed to the wicked and dangerous seductiveness of Eve, who yielded to the temptations of the serpent. These primal models recur in a wide range of mythical figures: woman is in turn sorceress or initiator, placed on a pedestal or sacrificed. Sometimes good and evil are blended together in images of ambivalent women in whom innocence and seduction are subtly fused.

The Love Charm, **German School**, fifteenth century, oil on panel, 9 ½ x 7 in. (24 x 18 cm), Museum der Bildenden Kunste, Leipzig

Venus
of Willendorf

◇◇

Discovered in 1908 in Willendorf in Lower Austria, this limestone statuette can be classified as a Paleolithic Venus, carvings that tend to be exceptionally corpulent, a characteristic often interpreted as a symbol of fecundity. Some historians have maintained that these female figures testify to the veneration of an all-powerful female divinity or mother goddess in Paleolithic societies, where it would have been associated with a matriarchal system, as in certain primitive tribes. These societies disregard the respective functions of the two sexes in procreation. Woman—considered as the unique possessor of power over the reproduction of the species—was associated with the revival of life and thought of as sacred. However, theories establishing correlations between such figurines and the worship of fertility or a mother goddess cannot by their very nature be based on written sources and are therefore impossible to verify scientifically.

Perhaps more simply these statuettes were used as magical amulets for women intent on becoming fertile. More recently, other historians have proposed they should be envisaged as an outlet for female self-representation, not only as an object of desire, but also as mistress of her own desire—somewhat redolent of works by contemporary women artists such as Louise Bourgeois (see p.22), Sophie Calle (see p.32), and Cindy Sherman.

Inanna-Ishtar

The cult of Inanna was one of the most fervently observed cults in the ancient Middle East. The Sumerian goddess of love, fecundity, and combat, she was embraced by the Babylonians under the name Ishtar. Her foot planted triumphantly on a lion's back, she is portrayed wearing imposing headgear made of horn and is draped in lapis lazuli jewelry. A passionate but dangerous lover, she transcends every social genre and code, and embodies the devastating force of desire when it surges out unconstrained. As so often in ancient pantheons, she is a hermaphrodite divinity who seduces women no less than men.

Among the Sumerians, the raw, destructive life force within her is expressed in unbridled sexuality, by conquests often achieved by trickery, and by outbursts of rage that lead her to exact terrible revenge on anyone who resists her. Having no truck with rules of civilization that constrain and channel, she is a prototype femme fatale, a dominatrix and mistress of her own body. Such an overflowing vital force nevertheless plays a role in the cosmic religion: Inanna is honored every year at a sacred wedding feast. The whole society gathers for a ceremony at which the king marries one of the priestesses of the goddess so as to ensure that the community remains productive and prosperous.

A guardian goddess, Inanna combines many of the contradictory principles of femininity that we will see laid at the door of any number of women in love in the course of this volume. Coming early in our anthology, she can be compared to Aphrodite in the Greek world and to Venus in the Roman.

The Venus of Urbino, **Tiziano Vecellio, known as Titian,** 1538, oil on canvas, 46 ¾ x 65 in. (119 x 165 cm), Galleria degli Uffizi, Florence

Venus

Of all female nudes in the history of painting, *The Venus of Urbino* is probably one of those who has commanded most attention from writers. Openly parading her nudity, the goddess of love, languishing on a bed, has always been seen as eminently dangerous. The gesture she makes with her left hand—borrowed from Giorgione's *Sleeping Venus* (see p.40-41)—has been the object of especial comment. Whereas this gesture might be natural and spontaneous in a person sleeping, it is conscious and perhaps provocative made by a woman in the waking state who is shown turning an unflinching and somewhat languorous gaze on the viewer. The roses in her right hand symbolize the pleasure the woman is affording herself. It is then no surprise that this painting has aroused astonishment, indignation even.

In the nineteenth century, on his travels, the American writer Mark Twain expressed his reaction in these terms: "You enter, and … there, against the wall, without obstructing rag or leaf, you may look your fill upon the foulest, the vilest, the obscenest picture the world possesses—Titian's *Venus*. It isn't that she is naked and stretched out on a bed—no, it is the attitude of one of her arms and hand. If I ventured to describe that attitude, there would be a fine howl…. " It is thus tempting to equate our Venus with a courtesan, for whom such an openly erotic gesture would be understood as an invitation to pleasure.

The presence of the puppy, a symbol of fidelity, and of myrtle, a figure of enduring love, however, both plead instead in favor of a conjugal context. This is accentuated by the two maidservants leaning over the wedding chests in the background. Venus might then embody a bride thinking about her husband and surrounded by symbols that foretell of their union. Her autoerotic activity might then be explained by the belief, widespread among physicians and theologians in the sixteenth century, that female masturbation was an aid to procreation.

It would seem that the main intended recipient of this picture, acquired in 1538 by Guidobaldo Della Rovere, future heir to the duchy of Urbino, was in fact a young woman. His wife, Giulia, whom he had married four years earlier, had reached the age at which their union might be consummated. For Giulia, then, the picture would represent a kind of model of ideal behavior in her triple role as lover, wife, and mother. Yet, even if this defuses the provocation and dangerous "obscenity" of this Venus, she nonetheless loses little of her undeniable erotic power.

Sleeping Venus (The Dresden Venus), **Barbarelli da Castelfranco, known as Giorgione,**
c. 1508–10, oil on canvas, 42 ¾ in. x 69 in. (108.5 x 175 cm), Gemäldegalerie, Alte Meister, Dresden

Venus

Mars and Venus,
Sandro Botticelli,
1483–84, distemper on
wood, 27 ¼ x 68 ½ in.
(69 x 174 cm),
National Gallery, London

The love between Mars and Venus, as described by Ovid and Homer, is well known.

Here the god of war is shown dozing on a crimson mantle. His half-naked body contrasts with Venus, neatly attired in an elegant white dress. In comparison with his alert and attentive lover, Mars looks weak and vulnerable. Four fauns are playing with his weapons, yet fail to disturb his slumbers. Not even the wasps buzzing around his face or the triton blowing a conch into his ear can rouse him from his torpor. Such are the consequences of lovemaking: it reduces the most bellicose of all the Olympian gods to the state of a gentle and inoffensive creature. The goddess's victory could hardly be more complete.

Certain historians have suggested that this painting commemorates a wedding, while others have identified analogies between the divine couple and Guiliano de´Medici and Simonetta Vespucci (with the wasps, *vespe* in Italian, evoking her family name and coat-of-arms), lovers whose lives ended tragically. It is true that Venus and Mars are shown in an attitude similar to that adopted by couples on Etruscan sarcophagi, but the surrounding landscape, dotted with bay trees, a symbol of peace, might equally refer to the city of Florence during the rule of Lorenzo de´ Medici (the association being between *lauro* and Lorenzo), since this was a period of serenity in which love had clearly triumphed over war.

The picture evokes the duality between hate and love and between war and peace, as personified by Mars and Venus. This symbolically complex work probably exalts the type of love explored by Neoplatonic philosophers and poets. In that conception, spiritual love, here embodied by Venus, should be dominant over the physical, as represented by Mars, not by force but by the preeminently "feminine" power of gentleness. More broadly, the picture appears as an allegory of the triumph of love over war, of the victory of harmony over discord.

Danäe

◇◇

According to antique tradition, Danäe was locked up by her father in a bronze tower because an oracle had predicted that he would be killed by his own grandson. Jupiter, however, turned himself into a shower of gold, entered the prison, and in this form performed coitus with the young woman.

Danäe is an ambiguous figure par excellence, the embodiment of both virtue and sexuality, of chastity and depravity. Though in medieval tradition she was occasionally equated with the Virgin, she is generally regarded as a venal female who succumbs to the temptation of lucre. Boccaccio even accused her of being meretricious and money-grabbing.

In this picture, Danäe is shown offering herself to Jupiter. Legs open, a smile playing on her lips, she gazes longingly at the shower of gold on her almost naked flesh. The way her fingers play with the bedclothes might also have sexual connotations. Furthermore, the medieval motif of the alcove of love (with the half-drawn hanging) is a further allusion to sex. Here, Danäe presents the absolute embodiment of the pleasures of love. The harmony between the young woman and Cupid, the god of love, and the manner in which their gestures echo one another all confirm Danäe's readiness. Still, everything in this painting is indicative of sensuality and love: the unmade bed, Danäe's golden curls tumbling over her shoulder and down onto her breast, her delicate, pearl-white and rather soft flesh, her yielding expression—right down to the putti in the foreground, one sharpening a golden arrow supposed, according to Ovid, to strengthen love.

Yet, as she gathers up the gold falling from the sky in the cloth covering her, this delightful and ostensibly innocent darling is clearly not quite exempt from Danäe's sulfurous reputation. Taking Correggio as his starting point, this aspect is accentuated by Titian, who gives the theme a still more parodic and erotic twist by replacing Cupid with an elderly maidservant unambiguously prey to rapacity. As for Tintoretto, he was to paint Danäe punctiliously collecting up all the gold coins. From amorous young woman to venal courtesan is, it seems, but a short step.

Juno

◇◇

From one angle, Juno is the mythological archetype of the jealous, possessive, and grumpy wife. Married to Jupiter, with whom she reigns supreme on Mount Olympus, she constitutes a constant danger to all those who catch the eye of her flighty spouse.

Tirelessly, she torments Io, causes Semele to be incinerated, prevails upon Diana to kill Callisto, and does her best to prevent Leto giving birth. Her anger is even directed at the offspring of Jupiter's adulterous liaisons, in particular Hercules, son of Alcmene, since the "twelve labors" were originally her idea.

Juno's physique may be noble and majestic, but she loses the beauty contest in which her rivals were Venus and Minerva: the designated referee, the Trojan, Paris, chooses the goddess of love instead. To avenge this slight, during the Trojan War Juno joins the side of the Greeks, her anger having a determinant effect on the course of events.

In this image, the master of Olympus seems completely subjugated—evidence of the power of this woman-cum-mistress. The goddess stands, proud and imposing, her breasts pointing toward her husband, while Jupiter sits on the marital bed, striving to attract her attention. The scene is not without a dose of humor.

The frescoes decorating the ceiling of the Farnese Gallery in Rome belong to a decorative ensemble that features many mythological couples. Playfully expressed, the point is often to show the women and men swapping roles. More broadly, the whole iconographic program is centered on the celebrated Virgilian theme of "*Omnia vincit amor*," "Love conquers all." Under the influence of love, even the greatest gods and heroes—here Jupiter, but Hercules too—are no longer quite themselves. If such a representation of female "power" would have raised a smile among Carracci's contemporaries, it is because it seemed unusual, counterintuitive, ridiculous even—a clear indication of the predominant mentality of the period.

Jupiter and Juno (detail), **Annibale Carracci,** 1597–1600,
13 x 15 in. (33 x 39 cm), fresco, Palazzo Farnese, Rome

Psyche

At the beginning, Psyche is a girl whose exceptional beauty frightens off all potential suitors. Her anxious father consults an oracle that commands him to abandon his daughter, dressed as if going to her wedding, on a rock. Alone at the top of the mountain, Psyche suddenly feels herself lifted up into the air and borne off by the wind into a valley where she falls into a deep sleep. This is the moment Maurice Denis has chosen to illustrate in this first painting. On waking, Psyche finds herself in the garden of a glorious palace. There, every evening, she is visited by a man who claims to be her husband. He satisfies her every desire, but asks her never to try to see him on pain of losing him forever.

Though Psyche is happy, one night she yields to curiosity. Holding a lamp over her mysterious spouse while he slumbers, she discovers his identity: he is the god of love himself. This is the episode shown in the second illustration. Perturbed by his beauty, she allows a drop of oil to fall on the young man and he immediately runs off. In despair, our Greek heroine scours the world for news of her lost beloved. Many other ordeals follow, ending finally with Psyche's apotheosis on Mount Olympus and her wedding to Cupid.

Recounted by Apuleius in the *Golden Ass*, this fable also serves as a metaphor for the human soul as it aspires toward the divine (*psyche* means soul in Greek). The ordeals that Psyche has to undergo can thus be interpreted as stages in a mystical initiation or spiritual journey. A deeply devout man, the painter in all probability knew of this aspect of the myth. Finally, on a third level, one can see the difficulties endured by the young girl as she searches for Cupid as a reflection of the obstacles and dangers that threaten all those who dare to embark on a love affair.

The present works are part of the *Cycle of Psyche* (1909, State Hermitage Museum, St. Petersburg), which adorned the music room in a Moscow residence belonging to the art collector, Ivan Morosov.

The Abduction of Psyche and The Curiosity of Psyche, Maurice Denis, 1909,
oil on canvas, 28 ¼ x 19 ¾ in. (72 x 50 cm), State Hermitage Museum, St. Petersburg

Eva Prima Pandora, **Jean Cousin the Elder,** c. 1550,
oil on panel, 38 ¼ x 6 in. (97 cm x 15 cm), Musée du Louvre, Paris

Pandora

◇◇◇

F ashioned from clay by Hephaistos, Pandora—like Eve—proved a poisoned chalice for mankind. If Eve was responsible for humanity being driven out of earthly paradise, then it was Pandora who opened a jar from which evil escaped into the world. These two primeval figures, one biblical, the other mythological (Hesiod, mid-seventh century BCE), have forever linked womankind with seduction, love, danger, and malevolence. One encourages her husband to taste of the Forbidden Fruit; the other deploys just as much charm to persuade Epimetheus to marry her despite his brother's warnings.

Here, Jean Cousin combines them in a single splendid specimen, the very prototype of the dangerous woman, an amalgam of the attributes of both Eve and Pandora. The apple branch she holds between her fingers and the snake rolled up her left arm hint at Eve. But, blessed with a Greek nose and feet, she can also be identified as Pandora—in particular thanks to the pair of vases: one containing all that is good, the other all that is bad. Her left hand rests on the vase with all the good, keeping it shut. In the composition as it originally appeared, black smoke and genii issued from the "evil" red vase behind her. These have faded over the years.

This slinky creature is also redolent of a nymph or of the goddess of love. Offering her splendid nakedness to our contemplation, she is reminiscent of many a Venetian Venus stretched out in a landscape or interior (see *The Venus of Urbino*, p. 38).

The iconographic proximity with the goddess of love exacerbates her powers of attraction. Sin and seduction here rub shoulders with death: the incarnation of alluring evil, the beautiful *Eva Prima Pandora* rests one hand (the one holding the branch of the apple tree, an allusion to original sin) on a skull. Is this a warning against the fatal consequences of lust? Things are by no means so clear. For, if it tells the beholder that the responsibility for our first sin should be laid firmly at the door of womanhood—a "femme fatale" in that sense—the very beauty of Jean Cousin's depiction nonetheless beguiles us. The danger of woman here merges with the blandishments of painting.

Ariadne

◇◇

Seduced by Theseus who had come to Crete to do battle with the Minotaur, Ariadne, the daughter of the king of the island, helps the young hero to escape from the labyrinth in which the monster dwells. She gives him a ball of string which he is to unroll as he makes his way through the labyrinth so that, having slain the beast, he can follow it back to the entrance and make his escape.

The victorious Theseus sets sail for Crete with Ariadne, but he soon abandons her during a brief stay on the island of Naxos. "Hardly having left her dreams, she suddenly finds herself all alone on a deserted beach. Oblivious, the young man has raised the sail and casts his promises to the wind! And the daughter of Minos follows him from the rocks with despairing looks." (Catullus).

This is the episode in the story depicted by Angelika Kauffmann. The legendary princess is shown on the seashore, prey to a hopelessness wonderfully conveyed by her expressive and dramatic gestures. At her feet, a weeping Cupid adds to the pathos of the scene.

The theme of the betrayed heroine particularly interested this artist, who also painted Sappho and Dido, as well as other examples of suffering women, such as Penelope and Calypso (see p.78). Like Ariadne, all these women endured the absence, temporary or final, of the being most dear to them. All were abandoned, left to their loneliness. Perhaps this theme of loss finds an echo in the life of an artist who had lost her mother in early youth.

Even absent, Theseus is to an extent still the principal subject of the picture and it is he who governs the young woman's destiny. The myth actualizes the dangers to which women expose themselves when, following the inclinations of the heart, they forget certain virtues traditionally associated with womanhood, such as obedience and submission. Ariadne is "punished" for having turned a deaf ear to the advice of her father who was persistently against her union with Theseus.

Ariadne's existence is determined by the men she encounters. Deserted by one man, she is rescued by another: encountering her on Naxos, Dionysus throws her bridal crown so high into the heavens that Ariadne is transformed into a constellation. Subsequently he made her his wife. Beyond the moving fable it retells, Angelika Kauffmann's picture thus advances a thesis on the female condition.

Dido

◇◇◇

While on his epic journey through the Mediterranean, the Trojan hero Aeneas reaches Carthage, where he is welcomed with open arms by its queen, Dido. At the instigation of Venus and Juno, they become lovers, but a jealous suitor pleads with Jupiter to get rid of Aeneas, who promptly makes up his mind to go and settle in Italy instead. Thus abandoned, Dido falls on Aeneas's sword and kills herself. The whole story is told in Virgil's *Aeneid* (IV, 504).

This elegant and delicate painting is most probably a panel that once decorated a *cassone* (a wedding chest), like the one appearing in the background of *The Venus of Urbino* (see p.38). A typical piece of medieval and Renaissance furniture in Tuscany, a *cassone* would have been ordered by the husband-to-be or the parents of the fiancée. Usually, the bride would store part of her trousseau (fabrics, dresses, embroidered linen) in these trunks, which were designed to be prominently displayed

The Suicide of Dido,
Liberale da Verona, early
sixteenth century, oil on wood,
16 ¾ x 48 ½ in. (42.5 x 123.2 cm),
National Gallery, London

in the bridal chamber. As with birthing trays and engagement caskets, *cassoni* were subject to a specific iconography, for the most part mythological, historical, or biblical, with scenes that stress the virtues incumbent upon the engaged couple. Often the legends shown have connections with marriage or family history, though a *cassone* could also feature cruel scenes, such as fathers killing their daughters, men slaying their wives, suicides, etc. This type of subject is probably explained by the then prevalent taste for adventure, but also by the admiration for docile women.

One should, though, be wary of caricaturing the patrician society of the time. For a woman, the dowry she received on her marriage was in fact a source of power, because only part accrued to her husband. Thus, when it came to choosing a husband or a convent for her daughter, a mother also had rights, insofar as a share of her own dowry would be transferred to her daughter's dowry in the future. Moreover, a married woman would in general maintain close links with her family, bonds which she encouraged her sons to keep up. Thus women played a key role in their sons' development into adulthood. Such factors introduced a note of flexibility into the rigid patriarchal system.

The Shades of Francesca da Rimini and Paolo Malatesta
Appearing to Dante and Virgil, **Ary Scheffer**, 1855,
oil on canvas, 67 ¼ x 94 in. (171 x 239 cm), Musée du Louvre, Paris

Francesca
da Rimini

◇◇◇

Paolo and Francesca form one of the great mythical couples of European literature. Forcibly married to Gianciotto Malatesta, an unprepossessing and difficult man, Francesca fell for the charm of her husband's younger brother, Paolo. After spending the evenings reading tales of chivalry, they end up avowing their love. When their liaison is discovered, however, Gianciotto, insane with jealousy, stabs them both.

Ary Scheffer, who had done a great deal to ensure the triumph of Romantic painting at the Salon de Paris of 1827–28, possessed a penchant for dramatic subjects. He here illustrates a passage from Canto V of Dante's *Divine Comedy*, in which the poet, accompanied as ever by Virgil, encounters the shades of lovers condemned to the torments of hell for succumbing to adulterous love. This star-crossed couple inspired other artists, including Ingres and Delacroix, but none mixes sensuality with mysticism quite like Scheffer. Their luminous, entwined bodies appear to surge up from the black depths through which they float ethereally. Merging into one, they represent two passionate souls that are joined by death in an eternal, intense embrace.

This picture can be correlated with the development in the late eighteenth century of a literature of pre-Romantic sensibility that placed emphasis on the drama, tragedy, and impossibility of love, on strong emotions, on the poetry of tears—as in Bernardin de Saint-Pierre's *Paul et Virginie*, for example, or in the British Gothic novel—from which a taste for macabre eroticism filtered into painting at the turn of the nineteenth century.

Following pages:
Death of Francesca da Rimini and Paolo Malatesta, Alexandre Cabanel, 1870, oil on canvas, 6 x 8 ft. 4 in. (1.84 x 2.55 m), Musée d'Orsay, Paris

Romeo and Juliet, **Louis Boulanger and Achille Devéria,** 1827,
illustration for *Souvenir du théâtre anglais à Paris,* print, 169 ¼ x 118 in. (430 x 300 cm),
Bibliothèque de l'Arsenal, Paris

Juliet

◇◇

Against the backdrop of the tenacious rivalry between the families of the Capulets and the Montagues in Verona, Romeo, heir to the second of these clans, and Juliet, daughter of the opposing family, meet at a ball and fall madly in love. They marry secretly in the hope that their union might reconcile their families. But, following a fracas, Romeo kills Tybalt, a Capulet, and is condemned to exile. Juliet's parents decide that their daughter should marry Count Paris with all possible haste. Seeking advice from a Franciscan friar, the girl alerts Romeo by letter that she is going to swallow a potion that will make her appear dead. In this way her body will be taken to the Capulets' vault from which she can be rescued by her lover. The funeral proceeds as envisaged, but the message never gets to Romeo. So, mistakenly believing that Juliet has genuinely died, Romeo hurries to the tomb of his beloved and downs a flask of poison. Juliet awakes to discover her lover dead and commits suicide in her turn with Romeo's dagger.

The composition of this print was based on performances by the English Theatre Company in Paris. The image adapts Shakespeare's drama to Romantic sensibilities: the theatrical backdrop, the half-light, the contrast between Juliet's white robe and Romeo's dark attire all accentuate the poignancy of the two lovers' tragic end.

Deveria et Boulanger delt

Shakspeare   Romeo et Juliette . Acte 5 scene derniere

The Death of Ophelia, **John Everett Millais,** 1852,
oil on canvas, 30 x 44 in. (76.2 x 111.8 cm), Tate Britain, London

Ophelia

◇◇◇

This depiction by Millais of the tragic fate of Ophelia as she sinks below the waters is one of the most famous of all illustrations of *Hamlet*. The event does not appear onstage in Shakespeare's play, but is recounted with singular descriptive power by Queen Gertrude. Ophelia, when she learns how her lover Hamlet has murdered her father, Polonius, loses her mind and drowns herself in a river: "There with fantastic garlands did she come/Of crowflowers, nettles, daisies, and long purples." Ophelia is the embodiment of the young, beautiful, but naïve and fragile woman, whose experience of romantic love can only have fatal consequences. Here love is inextricably linked to death, youth, and beauty—the favorite subjects among Pre-Raphaelite artists, who worked in an era when the matrimonial archetype was under severe strain.

The traditional institution of marriage, in which considerations of class and convention prevailed, was evolving into a union based on shared feelings. But this ideal too was vulnerable, since death (especially frequent in childbirth at the time) awaits to tear the couple asunder. Certain themes in Shakespeare thus appeared tailor-made to addressing such dilemmas.

The landscape in this work was painted from nature, while Millais—whom Baudelaire dubbed "an especially meticulous poet"—was staying in Surrey during the summer of 1851. The figure of Ophelia, however, was undertaken only later, in the studio in London. To do this, the artist developed a singularly original device: his model, Elizabeth Siddal—much appreciated by Pre-Raphaelite painters—posed stretched out in a bathtub heated by lamps. In fact, the work is as naturalistic in the depiction of the plants as in the treatment of the girl's face and hands. One critic of the time noted how the sheer profusion of details, so lifelike and precise, accentuates the tragedy of Ophelia's death. But this picture, bathed in a glow that verges on the supernatural, also harbors a rich and complex symbolism, manifested in the choice of flora: pansies (standing for contemplation), forget-me-nots, daisies (innocence), and poppies (symbols of death). As for the character of Ophelia, she transcends any actual human model and becomes an icon of the tragic heroine prepared to sacrifice herself.

La mariée (The Bride), **Niki de Saint-Phalle,** 1963,
lace, 87 ½ x 78 ¾ x 39 ¼ in. (222 x 200 x 100 cm),
Musée National d'Art Moderne-Centre Georges Pompidou, Paris

La mariée (The Bride)

Niki de Saint-Phalle here offers a quite different vision of married women—a theme tackled many times by this artist whose favorite subjects are femininity and women's various "roles." Unlike her *Nanas*, who exalt the triumph of femininity, the *Mariées* (*Brides*) look sad, despairing even.

This original piece is closely related to its creator's personal history. Born into an aristocratic Catholic family and receiving a strict schooling, Niki turned her life into a long quest for individual and artistic liberation from accepted norms. In this sculpture, tradition and modernity echo one another. So deeply anchored in Western society, the conventional institution of marriage—here symbolized by the wedding dress and bouquet—is countered by an almost provocative and disturbing modernity, visible as much in the formal aspects of the work (in the use of materials such as papier-mâché, the plastic toys) as in the symbolic impact of certain details: the huddle of babies are joined by crabs, crocodiles, planes, revolvers, etc.

Such elements are of course in flagrant contradiction to the innocence of the blushing bride, rendering the piece at the very least uncomfortable to look at. Such unease, one might suppose, mirrors the life of the artist herself, a passionate woman split between love, joy, humor, her work, and her many sufferings.

Seductress
and Enchantress

From Antiquity on, woman has been associated with the use of artifice: makeup, finery, ornaments—in many societies, everything connected with adornment is seen as specifically female, and often as a threat. Because these extraneous, artificial, and deceptive charms perturb the senses and unsettle the judgement. More broadly, in the Greek symbolic system, in particular with Aristotle and Plato, physicality, sensation, and femininity are all closely interconnected. Meanwhile a venerable Judeo-Christian tradition places the feminine on the side of the flesh and the sensible—not on that of the mind and of knowledge, both domains of the masculine.

Accessories form part not only of a woman's arsenal of seduction, but of her power too. From the early days of Christianity, however, among the Fathers of the Church in particular, good is bound up with reason and evil with passion. The first lapse, Eve's fall, is caused by a woman heeding her desire rather than her reason. So strongly anchored in Western thought, this negative vision of the feminine has given rise to many figures immortalized by artists. Circe, Viviane, and Salome are but a handful of the countless women who deploy artifice to attain their ends, using deadly weapons such as potions and spells, enchantment, and sensuality.

The Siren, **John William Waterhouse**, c.1900, oil on canvas, 20 ¾ x 32 in. (53 x 81 cm), Sotheby's, London
Thanks to the magical sound of their lyres, flutes, and voices, the sirens would lure sailors on to the rocks where they would be shipwrecked. They would then proceed to eat the survivors.

Original Sin, **Michelangelo Buonarroti, known as Michelangelo,** 1508–12, fresco, 54 ¼ x 153 ½ in. (137.5 x 390 cm), Sistine Chapel, Vatican City

Eve

◇◇

The first to commit sin in the Judeo-Christian tradition, Eve can be seen as responsible for all the misfortunes of humankind. Led astray by blandishments of the serpent, Eve disobeys the prohibition of the creator and eats of the fruit of the Tree of Knowledge, offering it to her husband who tastes of it in his turn. Divine retribution soon descends and the couple is expelled from the Garden of Eden. On the fresco, Eve is seen hiding her face in shame. On the right, the brazen, culpable nudity of the couple who were once chased out of paradise contrasts with the superbly blossoming physique, illustrated on the left, that they possessed prior to the fall.

In representing original sin, artists tended to place Adam and Eve to either side of a fig tree or apple tree, round which the serpent coils. Michelangelo's approach is innovative in this respect: Eve is shown seated, with Adam standing. According to the account in Genesis, it is Eve who first yields to temptation; but here both succumb, Eve receiving the forbidden fruit from the serpent while Adam stretches out his hands eagerly in the direction of the fig tree. Nevertheless, in providing the snake with a female body and face, Michelangelo equates the diabolic animal and Eve, by the same token implying that temptation, the source of evil in the world, arose thanks to the "weaker sex." According to an enduring tradition with roots in both Ancient and Judeo-Christian beliefs, the male is associated with the mind, the word, and the spiritual, and the female with matter, flesh, and the physical.

Prevailing Renaissance theories regarded woman as incapable of knowing her limits, of controlling herself, and hence she is easy prey for irrational, ungovernable, and dangerous instincts. The figure of Eve, in opposition to that of the Virgin Mary, served as the preeminent vessel of this negative view of womankind.

From the Renaissance, there was a widespread tendency to use depictions of Adam and Eve as a pretext for the display of beautiful naked flesh. However, the nudity of our first parents—ostensibly supposed to convey a religious message and serve as moral admonition—proves ambiguous in that, rather than dissuading the viewer from the dangers of the flesh, it might instead act as an advertisement for them and arouse erotic feelings. It is this ambivalence that underpins all representations of Eve: in presenting a dangerous woman, they necessarily entail a further danger—that of the erotic power of the image.

Bathsheba

O ne evening, looking down from the terrace of his palace in Jerusalem, King David spotted Bathsheba taking a bath in the open air. Overwhelmed by her beauty, and his desire aroused, he had her sent for and debauched her.

Francesco Salviati's approach in these frescoes illustrating the biblical story is as aesthetic as it is original. In the first, Bathsheba is the naked young woman bathing and surrounded by maidservants, similarly unclad. On the right, David, recognizable from his crown, observes the beauty he covets from his window. This elegant composition is characterized by an elaborate architectural backdrop, while its soft colors and light, delicate tone are in keeping with the sensual femininity of the scene.

In the next fresco, Salviati shows Bathsheba ascending the staircase on her way to her rendezvous with the king, reiterating the same figure three times in different attitudes. The device of representing successive sequences in the same image by repeating one or more figures is rather old fashioned, more frequently found in the art of the Middle Ages. The trick here, however, is exploited by the painter in an entirely novel manner. Not only does the repetition present an opportunity to display Salviati's artistic mastery and knowledge of anatomy, but it also reveals an original exploitation of space. The spiral staircase with the figure ascending is a clever and innovative device. At the top of the image, in the chamber, the bodies of David and Bathsheba, embracing, their legs entwined and exchanging kisses, form an inseparable unit that materializes the bond between them. Yet this biblical fable is also an illustration of the disastrous consequences of irresistible female charm. Later on, so as to clear the way to take Bathsheba as his wife, King David was to dispatch the young woman's husband, the mercenary Uriah, on a mission which he knows will result in certain death. But divine retribution is not long in coming: the new couple's firstborn child will not survive.

Circe Offering the Cup to Ulysses, **John William Waterhouse**, 1891, oil on canvas, 57 ½ x 35 ½ in. (146.4 x 90.2 cm), Gallery Oldham, Oldham

Circe

Daughter of the sun, the sorceress Circe dwells in a palace on the island of Aeaea where she brews potions that transform unwanted visitors into animals. In *The Odyssey*, Homer recounts how, returning from the Trojan War, Ulysses (Odysseus) and his companions make landfall on her island. The members of the crew sent out to see the lie of the land are duly metamorphosed into beasts.

Some of them, transformed into wild boars, can be seen at the woman's feet in this picture. An embodiment of a dangerous and depraved femininity, Circe symbolizes humankind's baser instincts: deploying evil spells, she transforms man into animal to appease his carnal desires.

A painter with a fondness for femmes fatales, Waterhouse depicts Circe on the point of handing her magic potion to Ulysses. She is shown in all her malevolent grandeur: arms outstretched, chin raised, with a haughty look—Circe is majestic and imposing. The wily Ulysses, however, will render her drugs ineffectual. Protected against her spells by a potion prepared for him by Mercury, the hero, who is seen here reflected in the looking glass, soon forces Circe to return his crew to their customary state. He even manages to turn the tables on the sorceress: Circe falls in love with him, and, changing her tune completely, offers him advice as to his future travels.

Salome

◇◇

The daughter of Herodiade, Salome is the epitome of the seductive but cruel young woman. At a banquet organized for her birthday, her uncle, Herod Antipas, swears he will give her whatever she desires if only she will dance for him. After the performance, Salome, at the instigation of her mother, asks for the head of St. John the Baptist, who had been thrown into prison for denouncing the marriage between Herodiade and her late husband's brother. The saint is duly beheaded and his head presented to Salome's mother on a platter.

Gustave Moreau's interpretation in *The Apparition*—with its novel and bizarre notion of presenting the severed head of the saint levitating in Herod's palace—struck visitors to the 1876 Salon de Paris forcibly. It is difficult to pinpoint this scene—drawn from the imagination of the painter—within the biblical account. Perhaps the hovering face spurting blood and ringed by a halo appears to Salome before she makes her abominable demand, like a vision she finds impossible to ward off. Interrupting her dance, she feels "an immense shiver beneath the trappings of the festival and her nude body turns pale in the midst of her triumph" (Ary Renan). Perhaps, though, the biblical femme fatale has already ordered the beheading and this nightmarish vision represents the remorse and terror that seizes her and which she struggles in vain to dispel. The extreme refinement of the ornaments and the gentleness of Salome's face form a powerful contrast with the brutality and the cruelty of her actions. Against an Oriental backdrop inspired by the Alhambra in Grenada, and in keeping with the nineteenth-century taste for horror as a source of beauty, pleasure mixes inextricably with pain.

Medea

◇◇

Falling desperately in love with Jason, the sorceress Medea assists the hero in overcoming various ordeals and, using her supernatural powers, in purloining the Golden Fleece. Keeping the promise he had made her, Jason takes her as his wife, but subsequently falls for another woman, Creusa. Abandoned and betrayed, Medea, prey to uncontrollable jealousy, gives her rival a poisonous cloak. Once under way, her revenge knows no limits, and in a rage she slaughters the children she had by Jason.

In Delacroix's picture, the bodies of the two children and their mother, arranged as a pyramid, fuse into a single entity expressive of Medea's irrepressible wrath.

The dark, earthy backdrop of the cave evokes brutality and wicked passions, as do Medea's thick black locks, the shadow that falls over her face to hide her eyes, and, finally, her taut right arm and fist clutching the dagger. Her children twisting to escape her grasp, their terror-filled eyes further emphasize the barbarism of the act Medea is on the point of committing. The red and brown colors of the robe also convey the tragic heroine's murderous rage, and perhaps also, by anticipation, the blood that is soon to flow. Medea represents par excellence a woman destroyed by the flames of all-devouring passion.

A Fantastic Cave with Odysseus and Calypso, **Jan Bruegel the Elder, known as Velvet Bruegel,** c. 1616, oil on canvas, 13 ½ x 19 ½ in. (34.6 x 49.5 cm), Johnny Van Haeften Gallery, St James's, London

Calypso

◇◇

After being shipwrecked on Ogygia, Odysseus is rescued by the nymph Calypso, its queen. Infatuated with the hero, Calypso tries every trick in the book to keep him on the island. Deploying all her charm and wiles, to the point of offering him immortality and eternal youth, she keeps him trapped on the island for seven years. But Odysseus's heart remains faithful to his wife, Penelope. All day long he sits on the seashore, inconsolable, gazing out over the ocean, until one day Zeus takes pity on him. Dispatching Hermes, the messenger of the gods, he commands Calypso to allow Odysseus to return to his fatherland. Calypso helps the hero build a raft and summons up favorable winds. Odysseus departs the island, leaving the nymph alone with her sorrow.

The painter perfectly captures the enchanting atmosphere of Calypso's island, which resembles an earthly paradise. The two solitary figures are shown in a luxuriant landscape with an abundance of fruits, flowers, and animals: it is a fabulous Eden in which unblemished love can flourish. Calypso has placed a leg over one of Odysseus's, a motif that was frequent in the art of the Renaissance as a metaphor for the sex act.

The Temptress

◇◇◇

While living ascetically in the desert, St. Anthony was assailed by devil-ish temptations, some of which took the form of erotic visions. His sensuality aroused, the hermit burns with lust. Woman is here associ-ated with the weakness of the flesh and the demonic world.

Félicien Rops's interpretation of the episode is an unashamedly iconoclastic reading: Christ on the Cross is replaced by a voluptuous, naked woman. It is she who is adored, and, instead of the inscription "INRI" (for "Jesus of Nazareth King of the Jews"), one reads "EROS".

As the artist stated: "This is more or less what I had in mind; that Satan would be saying here to good old Anthony.... `I want to show you that you're mad, my honest Anthony, to worship abstractions! Your eyes should no longer peer into the blue depths of your Christ's face, nor into those of incorporeal Virgins! Your gods have followed those of Olympus.... But if the gods have departed, there remains Woman, and, with the love of Woman, the fecund love of Life.´

This *Temptation of St. Anthony* stirred up a huge scandal in 1878. As Edmond Picard—a great art lover who ran the review *L'Art moderne* and who owned the work—was one day to write to the artist: "for the *vulgum pecus*, unaccustomed to decoding your powerful and cruel art, you are all too likely to be perceived as a mere pornographer.... To untutored eyes, this grandiose art—in which the feminine essence that dominates our age, so prodigiously different from that of its predecessors, appears in types that only the perspicacious soul of a great artist is able to make manifest—must remain a closed book." Picard was to piously conserve the work in his private study, locked away in a little cabinet with a double door, like a holy picture.

Maja

◇◇

In eighteenth-century Spain, a *majo* was a street dandy who dressed in the height of fashion—just like his female counterpart, the *maja*, a fruit- or flower-seller. Originating among the lower orders of Madrid and towns in Andalusia, the *majos* and *majas* regarded themselves as the unadulterated representatives of the spirit of Castille, and thus as superior to the upper classes. An important component of contemporary Madrid society, their clothing fashions were sometimes imitated by members of the higher echelons.

If the idea of painting two pictures using the same model in the same pose on canvases of identical format was surprising and innovative enough in itself, it is all the more so when one recalls the scarcity of female nudes in early Spanish painting. Interest in such subjects seems to have been confined to the court and to works by foreign artists, Velásquez's *Venus with the Mirror* (National Gallery, London) being an exception, though, crucially, it depicts a goddess. In point of fact, the erotic, even provocative appearance of this *maja* arises precisely from the absence of any allegorical or mythological pretext. Unlike other nudes in Western painting, the model's face is that of a portrait. Goya seems to have deliberately eliminated all elements liable to make the subject look less profane: no luxurious backdrop, no bright lights—simply a couch, some crumpled bed linen, and the *maja* staring unblinkingly at the viewer.

Denis Diderot once observed that there is a yawning gap between a *nude* woman and one wearing no clothes, because nakedness can still be a garment, an ornament or adornment. Here, however, the woman shown is no "nude": she has simply undressed. It can scarcely be surprising then that some of Goya's contemporaries labeled it "obscene."

Even the most voluptuous women by Titian, Rubens, and Boucher always possess a certain something indicative of an ideal that transcends the human world. Something very different is at work here: with a piercing look that recalls sexual defiance and consciously placing her body in an attitude designed to create maximum effect, the woman depicted by Goya is no divine emanation.

Maja Desnuda (Maja Nude), **Francisco Goya**, c. 1800,
37 ½ x 74 ¾ in. (95 x 190 cm), Museo del Prado, Madrid

The Beguiling of Merlin, **Edward Burne-Jones,** 1874, oil on canvas, 73 ¼ x 43 ¾ in. (186 x 111 cm), Lady Lever Art Gallery, Port Sunlight, Merseyside

Viviane

◇◇

In *The Beguiling of Merlin*, love appears in a menacing light. The picture probably illustrates an episode from *Le Roman de Merlin*. Viviane, the Lady of the Lake, pronounces a magic spell that plunges Merlin into a deep sleep. Having succumbed totally to the allurements of the fairy, Merlin agrees to teach her all his knowledge of the arcane.

In this painting, it is the female figure, standing and with a book in her hand, who occupies the dominant position, while the reclining Merlin, vulnerable and submissive, gazes on, enthralled by Viviane's words, by his love for the fairy, and by the forest engulfing him. There is a close correlation between the picture's subject and its treatment by the painter: the experience of enchantment (*beguiling*) is illustrated by sinuously swirling curves—the drapery, Viviane's body, the vegetation—that ensnares Merlin in an inescapable net. The snakes in the fairy's hair remind one of the mythological figure of Medusa, who changed all who gazed upon her into stone.

Viviane is possessed of similar power. Fascinated by her enchanting gaze, Merlin is transfixed and stiffens—the composition resembles a "freeze frame." Immobilized and defenseless, he is a victim of feminine wiles. The female type created by Burne-Jones is not unlike Gustave Moreau's femmes fatales, such as Salome (see p.74).

This dreamlike work is probably also partially rooted in the painter's autobiography. In his correspondence, Burne-Jones suggests a parallel between Merlin's love for Viviane and his own feelings for a young woman with whom he had a relationship, Maria Zambaco, whose features inspired those of the fairy.

Scheherazade

◇◇

Betrayed by his wife, the king of Persia, Shahriyar, decides to exact vengeance by marrying a different virgin every day and having her put to death after the wedding night. To put an end to the massacre, the daughter of the grand vizier, Scheherazade, offers herself to the sultan. On the evening of the wedding, she begins to tell him a riveting story, but is careful to leave it unfinished. Desperate to learn how it goes on, Shahriyar affords her a stay of execution. Scheherazade continues for one thousand and one nights, at the end of which the sultan abandons his revenge. Captivated by the imagination and the storytelling talents of his new wife, he decides to keep her close by him forever. Intelligent and cultivated, Scheherazade is a positive incarnation of a woman who frees herself from male oppression by her ingenuity and mastery of language.

Georges Barbier was one of the chief figures in the art deco style, and of Paris life in the Roaring Twenties. A painter, illustrator, and fashion designer, his art blends exoticism with refined elegance and simplicity. He was influenced by Orientalism, the Indian miniature, the lines of Aubrey Beardsley, the colors of the painter Leon Bakst (best known for his collaboration with Diaghilev's Ballets Russes), as well as by Chinese lacquer and Greek vase painting. Much in demand as an illustrator for fashion reviews and society magazines, Barbier also worked on advertising catalogs and in the luxury goods market, as well as finding time to illustrate both the classics of French literature and erotic works. Endowed with an exuberant imagination, he also created sets and costumes for the theater, cinema, and ballet. In this illustration of Scheherazade in a performance by the Ballets Russes, Barbier's graphic art attains its acme, conveying all the energy and dazzling charm of Nijinsky's interpretation.

Emancipation and Transgression in Love

Ever since Western civilization has been predicated on the dominance of male power, more or less underhand and vigorous conflict between the sexes has been the rule. There exists an entire current of thought—from ancient myth to the "Querelle des Femmes," from the feminist and "queer" movements to unisex fashion—and a "lineage" of women, too, that have engaged in combating the patriarchal model.

Schematically, there are two ways of escaping oppression: women either adopt values and attitudes traditionally associated with virility—thereby fighting on male territory—or else they have to claim and assert specifically feminine qualities. The same applies in amorous relationships: images show on the one side aggressive, even belligerent females, who exert or try to exert their influence by force; on the other (more commonly, doubtless), women whose ascendency is due to their "feminine" charm, wiles, and refinements.

This duality, already appearing in Greek myth and present throughout the history of womankind, betrays the difficulty of defining woman otherwise than *in relation to* man. Simone de Beauvoir's coinage, the "second sex," captures this well: it is as if the female sex can only be thought of in contrast to—or in accordance with—some masculine benchmark. Finally, though, there is one further ideal that is met throughout the ages and in a great deal of art: the androgynous symbiosis, in which man and woman, while maintaining their "otherness," develop qualities of the opposite gender and so pave the way to a harmonious union.

Colette in *Fantasio*, anonymous, 1932
Divorced from her husband Henri Gauthier-Villars ("Willy") in 1906,
Colette had a number of liaisons with women before remarrying in 1912.
She is today considered an important figure in the quest for female emancipation in the early twentieth century.

The Death of Sappho (Sappho at Leucadia), **Antoine Jean Gros**, 1801,
oil on canvas, 48 x 39 ¼ in. (122 × 100 cm), Musée Baron Gérard, Bayeux

Following pages:
Sleep, **Gustave Courbet**, 1866, oil on canvas, 53 ⅛ x 78 ¾ in. (134 x 200 cm),
Petit Palais–Musée des Beaux-Arts de la Ville de Paris, Paris

Sappho

◇◇◇

The Greek poetess inspired by love, Sappho, is an emblematic example of a woman who transformed her passion into art. It is hardly surprising then that in the eighteenth century she became a favorite subject among a number of women painters of the caliber of Angelika Kauffmann and Élisabeth Vigée-Lebrun. Yet none showed her prey to the torments of love. A picture by Angelika Kauffmann (*Sappho*, 1775, The State Art Museum of Florida, Collection of the John and Mable Ringling Museum of Art), for instance, bathes in a gentle and sensitive atmosphere: a charming Cupid lays his hands delicately on the poetess's shoulder as she sits, serene, in a calm, meditative pose.

We are then a million miles from the passionate and ardent female here depicted by Gros. As with other artists of his time—Pierre-Narcisse Guérin (*Sappho on the Rock of Leucadia*, c. 1800, State Hermitage Museum, St. Petersburg); Jean-Joseph Taillasson (*Sappho at Leucadia*, 1791, Musée des Beaux-Arts, Brest), or, later, Gustave Moreau (*Sappho*, 1872, The Victoria & Albert Museum, London)—the painter focuses on the suicide of the poetess after she is abandoned by a lover, Phaon.

Sappho is shown at the very instant when, racked with despair, she throws herself into the waters from the summit of a cliff at Leucadia. With head thrown back and eyes tight shut, her profile, lit from behind, is picked out with a glowing line; the stormy night sky and the glaring moon exacerbate the tragedy of her death throes. The painter deploys all his talent in capturing the pain of a woman devoured by the fires of unrequited passion.

Beyond the violence towards herself, Sappho was dangerous in another way: she had always been suspected of lesbianism, and thus of being a woman whose sexuality transgressed the norm. Her name is the origin of the adjective, *sapphic*, meaning lesbian, as represented explicitly half a century later by Gustave Courbet in *Sleep*.

A model of poetic inspiration, expressive of love's despair, and the incarnation of a sexuality liberated from all convention, Sappho is a mythical figure full of contradictions, whose life story is an amalgam of love, art, and suffering.

Delilah

◇◇

Samson, a biblical figure renowned for his awesome physical strength, was in the end laid low by his love for a courtesan, Delilah. The epitome of female trickery and seduction, Delilah not only betrays her lover; she does so for money. Bribed by the Philistines, she succeeds in extracting from Samson the secret of his Herculean strength: it resides in his hair, which has never been cut since the day he was born. Having got him drunk and dozy, Delilah cuts off the hero's locks and delivers him into the hands of the Philistines.

With the loving attention for detail that characterizes his art, Cranach has meticulously painted every curl of hair, every jewel, the gorgeous cloth, the elegant drapery, each element of the landscape. He lays stress on the beauty and daintiness of the young woman, on her deceptively gentle face and attitude, in vivid contrast to the rugged demeanor of Samson, still sporting his armor. The delicate handling is also in keeping with Delilah's actions and with her skill in doing the devil's work.

Like Eve, Delilah provides a prime example of seductive wickedness, and in illustrating this scene many artists seem to be warning their fellow men to exercise vigilance with respect to women. Samson's face reposes on the breast of the young beauty he adores and by whom he believes he is loved in return. Faced with a woman's treachery, even the most powerful hero is impotent.

Salmacis

◇◇◇

This little picture by Gossaert illustrates one of Ovid's fables that is sometimes interpreted as a metaphor for the dangers of female power. The nymph Salmacis has fallen for the handsome young Hermaphroditus, son of Hermes and Aphrodite. She declares her love to him, but is rebuffed. Rejected, she hides in a bush and spies on him. The instant he wades into the waters of a spring of which she is the guardian spirit, she leaps on him, hugs him with all her strength, and begs the gods to join them together as one for all eternity. Her plea is granted.

Gossaert has chosen to depict the moment that the nymph, wearing an aggressive and determined expression, grabs Hermaphroditus. Taken unawares, the youth's resistance is all in vain. The background shows the outcome of this metamorphosis: a hybrid, a *hermaphrodite*, the fruit of the union between adolescent and nymph. Many art historians have compared this image to the iconographical *topos* of the "power of women" that enjoyed considerable popularity north of the Alps in the early sixteenth century, often appearing in images showing women getting the better of men. Phyllis straddling Aristotle, Delilah betraying Samson, Virgil and the princess, and Judith decapitating Holophernes are the most frequent illustrations of a woman causing a man's downfall. The moralizing message is the same each time: when a man is disarmed to this extent, when he is totally subjugated by feminine beauty and lust, love becomes harmful and destructive.

Things are, however, rather less straightforward in Gossaert's painting. If Salmacis most probably does represent a dangerous and lascivious temptress, an incarnation of the sins of the flesh, the point is not simply to warn man against feminine charm or desire: it is also a paean to love. The couple is not truly engaged in a struggle, appearing instead to be performing a harmonious, elegant dance. As a dual being representing the search for, or the return to, an original unity, in the literature of the time the hermaphrodite creature in the background acted as a frequent symbol of the union of perfect love. In this, it recalls the "androgynes" described by Plato in *The Symposium*. In the beginning, Aristophanes recounts, until Zeus severed them in two, humanity consisted of double beings of spherical form, man-man, woman-woman, man-woman (the androgyne). Since then, humanity has been reduced to looking for its lost half in a search for primeval unity, a theory that would explain the origin of homosexual and heterosexual desire alike.

Is it then the evocation of perilous female lust or of ideal love? If Gossaert's picture remains in many respects equivocal, then Spranger's approach stresses the frankly erotic nature of the scene. Hiding behind a tree, Salmacis is shown feasting her eyes on the spectacle of the young Hermaphroditus entering the bath. Taking on a part generally played in art by male protagonists, the nymph nevertheless remains an object of aesthetic or erotic contemplation, since—being portrayed from the rear—Salmacis unwittingly presents her nude body not only to the viewer, but also to the man who originally commissioned the work: when gender roles are reversed, things are never entirely unambiguous.

Hermaphroditus and Salmacis, **Bartholomaeus Spranger**, 1580–82, oil on canvas, 43 ¼ x 32 in. (110 x 81 cm), Kunsthistorisches Museum, Vienna

Omphale

◇◇

In the collective imagination, the name Hercules is above all a synonym for awesome strength. Here, though, the hero is shown as being under the thumb of a woman, Omphale, who was, according to the Syrian rhetorician Lucian of Samosata, Queen of Lydia. To expiate a sin, Hercules has been sold to her as a slave. For three years, he has had not only to execute Omphale's military orders, but to obey her every whim. Taking him as a lover, she forces the hero to dress up as a woman and spin wool. She meanwhile takes up the hero's cudgel and puts on his lion's skin, thereby inverting the customary positions of dominant/dominated.

In this picture, Hercules' virility is masked by a precious cloth. Perched on an ancient sarcophagus, an imposing-looking Omphale, draped in the lion's pelt she has purloined from her lover, pulls him by the ear. At the queen's feet, a lapdog nibbles at the skin, an echo of Omphale teasing Hercules. One possible meaning of this tragicomic depiction of Hercules, ridiculed and subjected to the thrall of woman, is to warn against the blandishments of the flesh.

Hercules' pose is also reminiscent of the Hellenistic statue of *Laocoön*, the paradigmatic expression of the pathetic in the history of Western art. According to the story in *The Aeneid*, Laocoön, together with his two sons, was strangled to death by serpents. Above and beyond the fable, then, even his attitude betrays downfall and humiliation.

Armide

◇◇◇

Boucher here represents an episode from *La Gerusalemme Liberata* (*Jerusalem Delivered*, 1581) by Tasso, a fictionalized account of the First Crusade. Alone among all the crusaders, the knight Rinaldo (Renaud) has remained insensitive to the captivating charms of the sorceress, Armida (Armide). Grievously offended, Armida performs a magic spell that makes him fall in love with her and holds him captive in her enchanted palace.

Rinaldo is shown languishing at her feet. Concealed behind a column, his companions, Carlo and Ubaldo, observe their friend closely. The Saracen beauty's charming demeanor, her head tilted slightly to one side, her delicate gestures, her smile, are scarcely designed to put one on one's guard. And yet this young thing has total mastery over a valorous crusader! Having placed his helmet and shield on the ground, the hero, overcome with adoration, has even lost his virility; with hand on heart, he reclines, utterly besotted, in a gracious, almost feminine attitude. Significantly, a few years later, Boucher reused the pose in a painting of Venus.

Rinaldo's face too looks womanish. This blurring of identities is an effect of Armida's attentions. Under her influence, Rinaldo has been transformed. He leaves off fighting and hence a part of him dies: Carlo and Ubaldo, Tasso tells us, hear him sighing so much that they are afraid "his heart will take flight and take up residence in Armida."

In the indescribable disorder of a scene in which putti clamber over fabrics of every kind, the vegetation, and the architectural elements, the picture cleverly captures the turmoil of love—a real shock to the system. Yet this configuration, in which man is subordinated to woman, is only one stage in Tasso's narrative: a necessary one for Rinaldo, as he seeks to regain his virility and learns, through various lessons of love, to master his desires. Armida's journey is to attain a more civilized, that is, no longer magical, femininity through marriage.

The danger of love, as illustrated in this seminal episode, is that of loss; but something can be gained too, since surviving the ordeal results in a more substantial, renewed self.

Angelica and Medor, **Toussaint Dubreuil,** c. 1580,
oil on canvas, 56 ¼ x 78 ¼ in. (143 x 199 cm), Musée du Louvre, Paris

Angelica

◇◇

Inspired by Canto XII of *Orlando Furioso* (1532) by Ariosto, a sixteenth-century Italian poet, this picture tells of the loves of Medor (Medoro), a Saracen knight of obscure origins, and Angelica, princess of China.

Wounded on the battlefield, Medor is tended by Angelica, who carefully bandages his wounds in a shepherd's hut. The princess, pursued from the very first canto of the epic by every knight she meets (Orlando, Sacripante, Ferraù, Rinaldo, Ruggiero), and who has hitherto rejected all these noble suitors with scorn, falls desperately in love with a common soldier.

Becoming lovers, they spend their time declaring their affection by carving their names on tree trunks and rocks. Their idyll culminates in a wedding that sanctions their relationship. In an act of independence, initiative, and feminine freedom, Angelica, an object coveted by all, refuses all the most attractive proposals and chooses a husband to whom she will not be subjugated. Thus, Angelica takes charge, as it were, of her emotional life.

In this work, her "power" expresses itself in the way the entire picture is dominated by the luminous and carnal presence of the young woman carefully observing what Medor is writing.

The next episode in the story is presented in the background. Orlando, who had stumbled across the "knots of love" formed by Angelica and Medor's entwined names, is shown approaching a shepherd who confirms his worst fears. Infatuated with the princess, he is devastated by the news: thus starts his great madness, "so terrible that its like will never be seen again." Prey to uncontrollable jealousy, the jilted lover is seized by a wild and destructive rage. Uprooting ancient oaks, Orlando becomes unrecognizable and wanders through remote lands.

The position of the two central figures patently lays stress on the inversion of traditional male and female roles. This reversal is more comprehensible in the light of a literary debate that started in the thirteenth century and which continued to exercise minds in the Renaissance and even later. Concerning the respective merits of the two sexes, this polemic was known as the "Querelle des Femmes" (the "quarrel about women") and set authors critical of women in opposition to others, such as Boccaccio and Christine de Pisan, who rallied to their defense.

Joseph and Potiphar's Wife, Master of the Legend of Joseph,
Dutch painter, fl. c. 1490–1500, one of a series of six tondos,
painting on oak, diam. 61 ¾ in. (157 cm), Alte Pinakothek, Munich

Potiphar's wife

This delicate painting presents a playful interpretation of the episode in the Bible that tells of Joseph's misadventures in Egypt. Sold by his brothers, Joseph becomes a servant of Potiphar, one of Pharaoh's officers, who entrusts him with running his household. But Joseph has the misfortune of catching the eye of his master's wife, and, more vexingly, of resisting her advances. One day, finding herself alone with Joseph, Potiphar's wife seizes him by his garment and orders him to lie with her. Joseph succeeds in escaping, but as he hurries off he drops his cloak. In the picture, the young woman is first represented naked, in an elegant bed with a red valance, trying to pull the innocent Joseph under the bedclothes while he struggles to get away. Soberly dressed this time, Potiphar's wife, humiliated and enraged at being rebuffed, is next shown taking her revenge. Standing before her husband and pointing at the robe she pulled off Joseph as he made his escape, she unjustly accuses Joseph of trying to seduce *her*. In the background, one sees Joseph being escorted to a dungeon.

This episode in Joseph's checkered existence is one of many in the Bible intended to impart a moral lesson—one not entirely devoid of humor, it has to be said—against female lust and its dangers.

Gala

◇◇◇

O n meeting Gala in 1929, Dalí fell head over heels in love with her. The view of the proud and somewhat tense face of this Russian woman, ten years his senior, immediately reduced him to a state of adoration. In that first instant, he was dazed, sure he had met *the* woman. He at once began to court her assiduously.

Twenty-five years old, Dalí knew nothing of love. At first irritated, Gala finally succumbed to the pranks and candor of this eccentric young man who worshiped her. Out walking with him one day, she declared: "My little one, we are never going to part from one another."

At the time, Gala was involved in a triangular relationship with Paul Eluard, her husband, and Max Ernst, her lover. She made up her mind to initiate Dalí into the ways of love, and they married three years later, leaving Eluard to his despair. Becoming Dalí's muse and unique model, her beauty is sublimated in paintings in which she is elevated to the status of a goddess or mythical figure, as in this work, where she appears in the guise of Leda, one of Jupiter's conquests.

According to Ovid, the king of Olympus took the form of a swan and seduced the girl on her wedding night. This union resulted in both Helen and Clytemnestra, and Castor and Pollux, all four emerging from a pair of eggs laid by Leda.

Whereas in the pictorial tradition it is generally the erotic potential of the myth that is exploited, Dalí's interpretation is very different. Painted shortly after Hiroshima was bombed, his *Leda Atomica* alludes to theories of contemporary atomic physics. In works by da Vinci, Michelangelo, Correggio, and Boucher, the swan caresses, envelopes the young woman, sometimes even copulating with her. Nothing of the kind here. In an illustration of the discontinuity of matter, neither Leda, nor the swan, nor the pedestal, nor the plinth, nor the sea touches anything else: everything is suspended, in levitation.

But the painting is above all a celebration of Dalí's unconditional love for Gala, this cold woman, deprived of what one could properly call beauty, who nonetheless managed to exert a mysterious pull on men. As the painter confessed, "I polished Gala to make her shine, making her as happy as possible, looking after her better than I did myself, because without her it would all be over."

Claude
Cahun

‹‹‹

The love life and art of the Surrealist poet and photographer Claude Cahun, born Lucy Schwob, have been the subject of much commentary. When only fifteen, she fell in love at first sight with Suzanne Malherbe, who later became her sister by marriage when Claude's father wed Suzanne's mother in 1917. Similarly an artist (painter and engraver), Suzanne took the pseudonym Marcel Moore and Lucy that of Claude Cahun, and they remained partners until the latter's death.

Such games on sexual identity went well beyond their choice of forenames: indeed a search for identity permeates Claude Cahun's entire oeuvre, which consists chiefly in self-portraits; and it can be read as a quest for an androgynous ideal that would transcend sexual divisions.

In this photograph, Cahun's reflection in the mirror is an example of her intense quest for the self through images. If the figure looking out at us, Cahun the artist, is readily identifiable, the *other* forms part of a self that hovers forever out of reach (the two faces seem to be moving away from one another), just as it eludes the viewer, whose eyes cannot meet the fleeting gaze reflected in the mirror.

The piece is also a reconfiguration of the subject of a woman staring into a looking glass that became popular at the end of the nineteenth century. The theme acquired special resonance in connection with female homosexuality, since the mirror—in which the subject's image is reversed—is particularly well suited to representations of sexual "inversion." This is still more relevant here since Claude's face is rendered extremely masculine. The portrait probably represents a quest for a synthesis between the sexes, at once within herself and in her relationship with Moore.

Through her personal mythology and art, the artist reiterates an archetype encountered in many cultures and periods, from the Greece of Antiquity, via ancient India, to today's "metrosexuals": primal androgyny. In rejecting a strictly feminine conception of woman, by incorporating the masculine, Claude Cahun forms part of the ongoing growth and emancipation of modern woman.

Tracey Emin

◇◇◇

The art of Tracey Emin—a celebrity in England thanks to TV and the tabloids—is among the most shocking produced by any woman today. From an early stage, she has turned her life story, which has been punctuated with painful events such as rape, attempted suicide, abortions, and the loss of a much-loved uncle who was decapitated in a car accident, into the principal subject of her oeuvre. With Emin, love is almost always accompanied by danger, provocation, tortured expressions of the self, or death.

In 1997, at the "Sensation" blockbuster show in Charles Saatchi's gallery, London, she unveiled a piece entitled *Everyone I Have Ever Slept With 1963-1995*. It took the form of a blue tent inside which appeared the names of all the artist's sexual partners, together with those, not only of the members of her family and her twin brother, but also of her two aborted infants.

Emin continued publicly to display her private life with *My Bed*, shown in the Tate Gallery during the Turner Prize two years later. This installation, with its soiled bedclothes, and the floor around it strewn with used condoms, cigarette packets, empty bottles of vodka, bloodstained knickers, and other detritus, whipped up a media storm.

By showing her bed in the state it was when she lay in it for days assailed by the idea of suicide due to problems in her love life, the artist turned herself into a kind of heroine of sexual suffering and its exhibition. If her series of neon lights, like the poetic *You Forgot to Kiss my Soul*, seem less provocative, they are nevertheless rooted in the same violently expressive and deeply human vein that characterizes Tracey Emin's art as a whole.

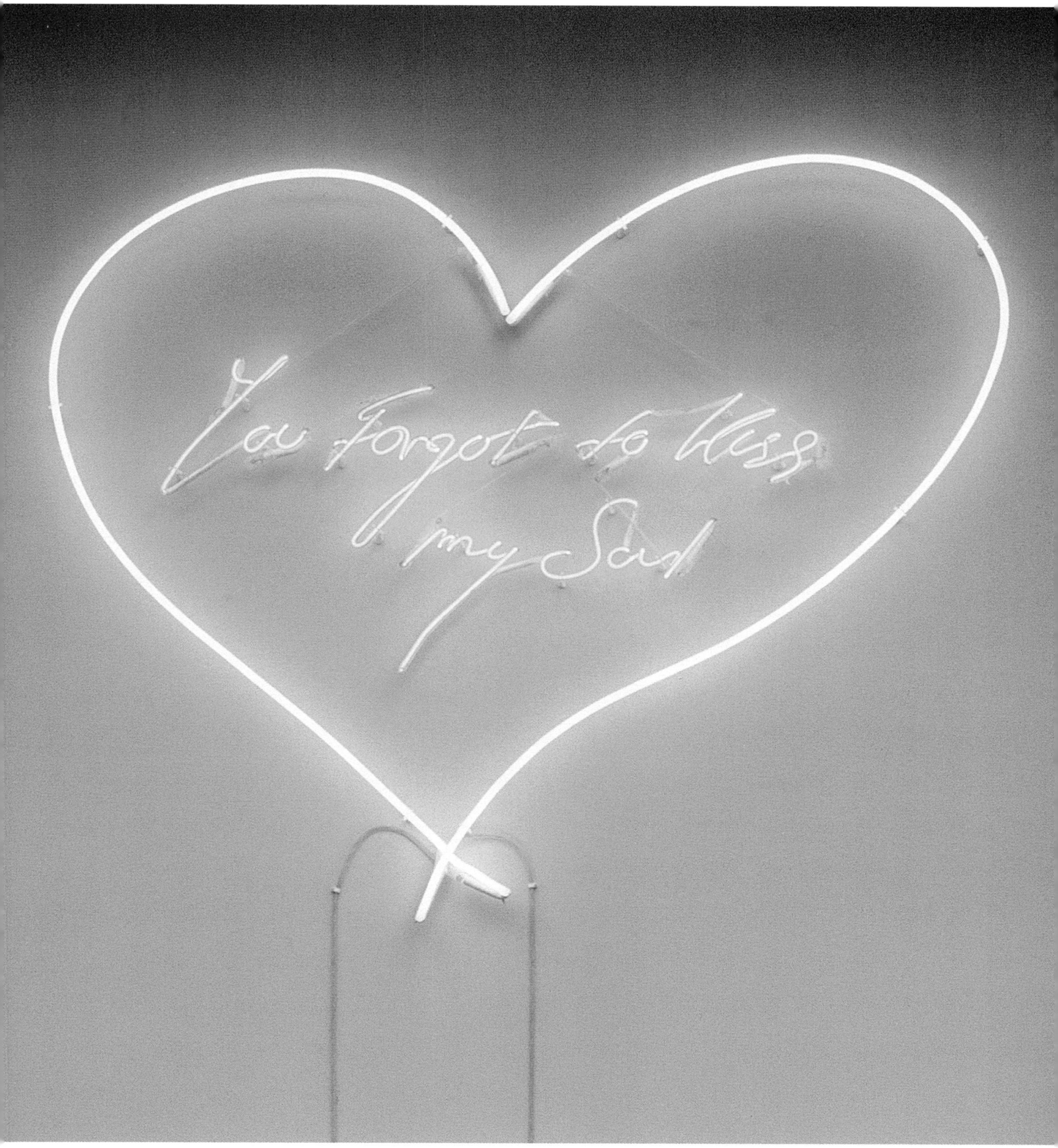
You Forgot to Kiss
my Soul

Women
and Power

History and mythology are full of female figures who made a crucial impact on cultural or political life, either because they themselves held the reins of government or because they played a decisive role as the wife or mistress of a king or ruler. Unlike some women who, as they enter politics, appear to put their femininity to one side so to speak, others exert an influence employing different means. Their preferred tool is love, real or feigned. This is the case with the great biblical heroines such as Judith and Esther, who used their beauty to save their people. In the First World War, the delectable Mata Hari gave her talents as a dancer in the service of espionage. Others, by arousing passion, destabilized whole nations: Wallis Simpson cost her dear Edward the British crown. Historians have commented on Marie-Antoinette's role in exacerbating the dissatisfaction of the French at the dawn of the Revolution. And then there is Helen of Troy, whose mere existence tipped the world over into war. Some, finally, by their perceived charm, generosity, or kindness, won the love of a nation: Eva Perón, Princess Diana, Jackie Kennedy.

Athalia (detail), **Xavier Sigalon,** 1827, 14 x 19 ½ ft. (4.2 x 6 m), Musée des Beaux-Arts, Nantes
Abandoning the Jewish religion, Athalia, the wife of the king of Judea, imposed the cult of Baal on Israel.
After the death of her husband and son, she eliminated all the princes of Judea so as to reign entirely on her own.

The Loves of Paris and Helen, **Jacques Louis David**, 1788,
oil on canvas, 57 ½ x 71 ¼ in. (146 x 181 cm), Musée du Louvre, Paris

Helen

◇◇

It was a woman, Helen, who sparked the Trojan War in which the Greeks were embroiled for ten years. Her beauty was exceptional and, when it came to marrying her off, her father was overwhelmed by the sheer number of suitors. Though Helen had favored Menelaus, king of Sparta, Venus had already promised her to Paris, a young Trojan who decided to take the beauty by force. It is this abduction that marks the start of the Trojan War, documented by Homer in *The Iliad*.

Exhibited at the Salon de Paris of 1789, this picture lifts the veil on the illicit love of Paris and Helen, an episode seldom represented by artists, who tend to prefer the scene of the abduction. With lowered eyes, betraying embarrassment or perhaps a feeling of guilt, Helen leans against her beau.

Some legends say that she was abducted against her will, but others claim that she was complicit and fell in love with the youth. The latter's passionate ardor is clear for all to see in his expression and reddening cheeks.

The image overflows with amorous allusions. On the left, on a column, a statue of Venus stands enthroned, and the goddess also appears on the medallion decorating Paris's lyre. To the right behind the bridal bed, a symbol of marriage, a crown of myrtle, hangs from one end of the screen. Beneath this crown, a bas-relief presents another legendary couple, Cupid and Psyche, embracing (see p.48).

Judith

◇◇

In the Bible, Judith—whose name simply means "the Jewess"—is presented as a paragon of civic virtue and, because she used her beauty to save her people, as an example of courage and daring. The victory of this heroine in slaughtering a tyrant illustrates the triumph of good over evil, and for Christians it prefigures the triumph of Christ over death. But Judith is also the incarnation of seduction, a fatal trap for any man beguiled by her charms.

The Israelite city of Bethulia is being besieged by General Holophernes. Bedecked in all her finery, the beautiful Judith visits the enemy camp with her maidservant. Holophernes soon succumbs to the bewitching spy, and, as he begins to feel drowsy, Judith seizes her chance and slices off his head.

This painting offers a realistic yet poignant interpretation of the biblical narrative. The absence of decor, the narrow focus, and powerful chiaroscuro dramatize the scene and pull the eye into the core of the action, Holophernes's head, from which spout jets of scarlet blood. The center of the picture is occupied by Judith's hand wielding a sword in the shape of cross, an allusion to the divine punishment being meted out to Holophernes. The bed he lies on resembles a butcher's block, but it might equally evoke a wedding bed—or a deathbed.

In Counter Reformation broadsheets advocating the destruction of heretics, Judith was often quoted as a model to be imitated.

Beyond the political and religious ramifications, though, for Artemisia Gentileschi the theme might well have possessed more personal resonance. The artist's identification with Judith can be deduced from a minor detail: the heroine wears a bracelet with medallions representing the goddess of chastity and hunting, Artemis, whose name echoes Artemisia's.

Perhaps, in this image of a biblical heroine punishing a man, the artist, who was raped at a young age, is attempting to cast out the violence of which she was a helpless victim. But it would be reductive to equate her creative power and the originality of her pictorial language solely with a desire to represent strong women who rebel against the female condition.

Esther

◇◇

Esther is the embodiment of the irresistibility of feminine charm. Having repudiated Vashti, Assuerus, king of Persia, chooses for his wife a young Jewess, Esther. In spite of the prohibition against entering the presence of the king without a summons, one day she appears before him, unbidden, to beg him to save some Jews sentenced to death. Extraordinarily, the king grants her request. Esther, who, like Judith, knew how to deploy her charms to save her people, is of course a Jewish heroine, but more generally her story harks back to the theme of the bewitching slave-girl whose beauty overwhelms and tames a tyrant.

Chassériau uses this depiction of Esther preparing herself for her first meeting with Assuerus as a pretext to delineate the allurements of naked female flesh. At this period in his career, the painter focused his aesthetic research on heroines from sacred and profane history. Esther's sinuous curves are clearly inspired by Ingres, but the warm, luminous colors, the full forms, the powerful physique, and radiant, majestic sensuality of the young woman are of a personal female type of the artist's own devising.

Seldom represented, the episode here puts one in mind of the closed world of the harem, allowing the painter to give free rein to a sensual evocation of an Orient inhabited by odalisques. The two figures flanking Esther, a maidservant and a eunuch, also form part of the exotic set—no more and no less than the jewels and accessories. Esther herself resembles a princess of the East, for example the favorite sultana described by Victor Hugo in the *Les Orientales*: "Tu n'es point blanche ni cuivrée/Mais il semble qu'on t'a dorée/Avec un rayon de soleil" (You are neither white nor coppery/Rather it seems you have been gilded/With a sunbeam).

Her raised arms, languorous air, and remote gaze, magnetizing the viewer, all accentuate the eroticism of a scene in which a naked young woman prepares to offer herself to her future husband. Though Chassériau takes his inspiration from the general iconography of women at their toilette, a theme thoroughly exploited in the Renaissance and ideal for a sensual description of a woman in her most private moments, his Orientalist approach gives it a novel twist.

The Suicide of Cleopatra Bitten by the Asp,
Giovanni Pietro Rizzoli, known as Giampietrino, sixteenth century,
oil on wood, 28 ¾ x 29 ½ in. (73 x 75 cm), Musée du Louvre, Paris

Cleopatra

◇◇

Cleopatra was a powerful woman indeed. Queen of Egypt (69–30 BCE), she was successively the wife of her brothers Ptolemy XIII and Ptolemy XIV, who sent her into exile. As mistress of Julius Caesar, however, she was to return to power and, with the assistance of Rome, strove to restore Egypt's hegemony over the Mediterranean. After the death of her lover, Caesar, she married Mark Antony, who offered to divide the East with her. Threatened by this confederation, Caesar's heir Octavian fought Antony and Cleopatra's troops at Actium, roundly defeating them. In order to save their honor, the only option for the defeated was to commit suicide. In Plutarch's version, Cleopatra first has Antony informed that she is dead. In despair at the news of his loss and humiliated at having shown "less courage than a woman," the general stabs himself. Cleopatra has him buried and persuades Octavian that she still wishes to live. Shortly afterwards, she orders an asp to be put in a basket of figs and, dressed in her full regalia, allows herself to be bitten in the breast.

Until the very end, Cleopatra controlled her own life and those of the men around her. She is for this reason a prototype of the dangerous femme fatale.

Taking a few poetic liberties with the literary tradition, Giampietrino represents Cleopatra naked. With her hair in plaits, a frequent hairstyle among followers of da Vinci, the queen is shown wearing nothing but her jewels: pearls in the ears and a pendant falling between her breasts. Her voluptuous curves are stressed, with one hip raised in contrapposto.

Displayed to all eyes, her beauty makes her death seem all the more heroic and striking. One hand on the basket, the other holding the death-dealing asp, Cleopatra averts her gaze as the snake strikes home.

Isabella
d'Este

◇◇

Daughter of Ercole I d'Este, duke of Ferrara, and of Eleonora of Naples, Isabella d'Este was one of the most famous art patrons of her time. At fifteen, she married Gian Francesco Gonzaga, marchese of Mantua, by whom she had eight children. Several paintings commissioned by the marchioness celebrate the perfection of their union. Devoting considerable sums of money to accessories of all kinds, Isabella was renowned throughout Europe for her beauty and excellent taste. Some princes even dispatched envoys to make drawings of her clothes and jewelry and have them reproduced. This veneer of grace and femininity, however, admirably captured by da Vinci in this sketch, concealed a charismatic and potent personality. As she herself declared: "Virile natures can be found even in our sex."

An acute political brain, on several occasions Isabella assumed the reins of government in the absence of her husband. Moreover she surrounded herself with a large court of literati, musicians, and painters, attracting some of the most eminent artistic personalities of the era, such as Perugino and Mantegna. The city of Mantua thus became a fertile and influential hotbed of the arts. With advice from various humanists, the marchioness in person helped to devise the iconography of several projects, in particular in her *studiolo* (private study), in this manner constructing an ideal image of herself and her marriage.

In this profile portrait—resembling a medal of a Roman emperor—da Vinci blends naturalness with idealization, presenting the marchioness as at once a paragon and a reality.

Agnès Sorel

Enthroned in majesty, wearing a crown and surrounded by her court of cherubim and seraphim, the supernatural beauty of Jean Fouquet's *Madonna and Child* is striking. Hieratic in her attitude, she has something of a Byzantine icon about her. As white as alabaster, standing out boldly against a red and blue ground, she resembles a statue, the folds of her mantle evoking the drapery that Gothic sculptors would carve in stone. The devout would see her bared breast, as with the motif of the Virgin nursing the Child, as a concrete image of the mystery of the Incarnation. A marker of triumphant maternity, this daring breast would verge on blasphemy, were it not for Mary's lowered eyes and humble, restrained expression. The danger is all the greater since her features reproduce those of Agnes Sorel, the first official mistress of the king of France, Charles VII, whose stunning beauty and influence over the sovereign's policies was amply reported at the time.

Here, as in many portrait drawings of the sixteenth century, one can identify the characteristic features of this royal favorite: high forehead, straight nose, small mouth, and delicate chin. Regarded in her lifetime as the loveliest woman in the kingdom, she lavished considerable sums on precious textiles, had her gowns bordered with marten or sable, her hair done up in elaborate styles, and invented a plunging, bare-shouldered neckline that was condemned by chroniclers of the period. She wheedled her way into the confidence of the monarch's advisers, and the king bestowed several estates on her, including the château at Beauté-sur-Marne, which earned her the nickname of the "Dame de Beauté."

Few works mix the divine and the human, the sacred and the profane to the degree of the Antwerp *Madonna*. The simplification of the forms and the hues, which verge on the abstract, sublimate the humanity of this Virgin, who is in truth a real woman tinged with a chilly eroticism. The paint substance is light, luminous, immaterial almost. Displayed here in all its lusciousness, Agnes Sorel's earthly beauty, in conjunction with the love she sparked in a king (and perhaps in the person who commissioned the work), is marshaled in a celebration, almost overwhelming in intensity, of divine beauty, love, and glory.

Madame de Pompadour

D rawn by the prince of pastellists, Maurice-Quentin Delatour, this portrait depicts a woman who, as first mistress then friend of King Louis XV, played a crucial role in the cultural and political life of the eighteenth century: Madame de Pompadour. This work, commissioned from the artist by the marquise herself, is based on a precise program. Seated at her desk in an elegant paneled study, Mme de Pompadour is attired in a sumptuous dress that immediately signals her rank and status. The floral motif points to her passion for flowers and gardens. Though the sitter's charms are much in evidence, she wears neither jewelry nor hair ornaments.

The aim of this intimate-looking portrait is to present the marquise in her guise as protector of arts and letters. The everyday objects surrounding her testify to her culture: the guitar on the couch and the score she holds in her hand evoke a taste for music. An engraving inscribed "Pompadour sculpsit" and Pierre-Jean Mariette's *Le Traité des pierres gravées* on the table illustrate her familiarity with the arts, while Guarini's famous play, *Il Pastor Fido*, alludes to the theater she had had installed for the king in the Petits Appartements. Among the titles on the console can be seen several fundamental Enlightenment works on science and literature: the *Encyclopedia*, Montesquieu's *On the Spirit of the Laws*, Buffon's *Natural History*, Voltaire's *Henriade*. As for the globe, it is a reference to the grandeur of France.

A close confidante of the king, Pompadour wanted to introduce the spirit of philosophical freedom that was blowing through Europe to a court that she found stiff and preoccupied with etiquette. If the king himself did not adopt these ideas as enthusiastically as she would have liked, the marchioness nevertheless played a major role not only in organizing court entertainments, but also in piloting the policies of Louis XV. Such at least is what this picture would have us believe.

If lacking in warmth, this luminous portrait remains a paean to an intelligent woman whose advice was listened to even by a king.

Isabella
Stewart Gardner

◇◇

Born into a wealthy and venerable family, at the age of twenty Isabella Stewart married the financier Jack Gardner. The young woman was far from blessed as a mother, however: her son died at the age of only two, and, following a miscarriage, she was advised against further pregnancies. She subsequently channeled her fabulous energies into traveling and then into assembling around her a coterie of aesthetes, artists, and intellectuals—notably Henry James and the painters Anders Zorn and Whistler.

The estate she inherited on the death of her father enabled her to devote herself entirely to her vocation: collecting works of art. In the process, she acquired some veritable masterpieces of painting, today preserved in the Isabella Stewart Gardner Museum, Boston.

Surprising in her artistic choices, Isabella was no less so in her life. Having lost all hope of motherhood when only twenty-five, she threw off all the conventions society imposes upon women of her condition. In her appearance, in her often eccentric notions, and in her love life, Isabella seemed almost to cultivate scandal as an art form. Her brazen behavior was legendary: she drove at breakneck speed, smoked cigarettes, decorated her hair with diamonds sticking up like feelers.

One day she persuaded the Boston Zoo to lend her two small lions for a few days and promptly paraded them up and down Commonwealth Avenue. On another occasion, at a concert, she was spotted handing out programs in front of the entrance to the auditorium in an effort to attract the attention of some musician.

Throughout her married life, she forged many intense attachments to other men. When forty-two, she had an adventure with the American writer Francis Marion Crawford, then aged twenty-eight.

Sargent places his model in front of a piece of delicate Italian brocade, showing the great American aristocrat from the front, full length, standing in a slightly stiff, dignified attitude. Her head ringed by a halo formed by the motif on the fabric, she almost looks, as Henry James put it, like a "Byzantine Madonna."

For the painter, however, the sittings were no picnic, as Isabella spent the whole time fidgeting. Her husband loathed the painting, remarking: "[The picture] is dreadful, but it does resemble you."

Wallis
Simpson

If there ever was a woman whose love life threatened the political stability of a whole country—a real one this time—it was surely Wallis Simpson, who, on becoming duchess of Windsor, sent shockwaves through the British establishment. When, in 1936, King Edward VIII announced his intention to marry "the woman he loved," a woman twice divorced, suspected of being an opportunist and a gold-digger, and who had been his mistress for several years, the country found itself on the brink of a constitutional disaster. As monarch of the United Kingdom, Edward VIII was also supreme head of the Church of England, and for this reason he could not marry a divorced woman, as the Church did not authorize remarriage for divorced people. If the king married Wallis without giving up his duties, the government would have been forced to resign, leaving a grave constitutional crisis in its wake. Since Edward VIII wanted Wallis at all costs, there remained only one solution: abdication. After the king stepped down, the couple married in June 1937, by which time Wallis was forty-two. She was never received by the royal family; they never officially accepted her, refusing her the title of "Her Royal Highness." The couple were guests of Hitler in 1937, and suspected of harboring Nazi sympathies, confirmed by some of their attitudes during the War.

The photographer captures perfectly here the anxious—and unsettling—expressions of the duke and the duchess alike.

Red Jackie, **Andy Warhol**, 1963,
silk-screen ink over acrylic on canvas, 40 ¼ x 40 ¼ in. (102 x 102 cm),
Andy Warhol Museum, Pittsburgh

Jackie
Kennedy

Jackie Kennedy is among the great mythicized females of the twentieth century, like Marilyn Monroe, Brigitte Bardot, Princess Grace of Monaco, and Princess Diana. Becoming first lady in January 1961, Jackie, wife of John F. Kennedy, and a victim throughout their marriage of his morbid adulterous tendencies, quickly acquired the status of an icon. Adulated, admired for her style and charm, imitated by society women the world over, she was immensely popular among the people. Canonized as an exemplary widow following the assassination of the president, she was toppled from her pedestal a few years later on becoming the wife of the Greek shipping magnate and billionaire, Aristotle Onassis. Considered by all as positively scandalous, their marriage unleashed a concerted torrent of hatred from the media and the public alike.

After the president was shot, Andy Warhol did no fewer than 302 portraits of Jackie. In the one shown here, the artist presents us with a positive image of a radiant Jackie, the incarnation of all the hopes that the mythical Kennedy couple embodied. Other portraits of Warhol show her in tears next to the bier carrying her husband's body, images of a lamenting widow that signaled the end to the sense of a new dawn that had gripped America in the Kennedy era.

The "Eternal Feminine"

Muses, victims, and femmes fatales

"The Eternal Feminine draws us upwards." The line that concludes Goethe's *Faust* Part Two exalts and ennobles woman, presenting her as a shining light that guides man as he ascends into the transcendental dimension. A foretaste of this exaltation emerged as early as the twelfth century, in the troubadours' cult of the lady.

Dante's Beatrice and Petrarch's Laura both represent this idealized feminine: placed on a pedestal, they serve as a bridge to a purified, spiritual love. In the same register, the Marian cult and the veneration of female mystical saints turn woman into a bridge to the divine. This fascination persists in literary salons and among the oracles of the Romantics. Yet this "eternal feminine" is not free from ambivalence: she also includes the femme fatale, wily and perverse—depraved, even.

Elevated to the level of goddesses, the dazzling creatures of the golden age of Hollywood movies—Ava Gardner, Elizabeth Taylor, Marilyn Monroe, or Rita Hayworth, to name but a few—were the objects of comparable idolatry. The same mythical image of woman recurs: a blend of the tantalizingly out of reach and the "vamp." Trapped in their image, the most popular of these supernatural beauties were often the most miserable. Just as, all too often, the creator's muse or the poet's inspiration remains chained to the man who adores her and wilts in his shadow.

It remains to be seen whether this "eternal feminine" is today a mere outdated stereotype, or whether it still resonates within our collective imagination and in the real world.

Phryne (detail), **Franz von Stuck**, c. 1917–18, private collection
Accused of debauching Athenian girls, the hetaera—courtesan—Phryne, a legendary beauty, was brought to trial, where she was defended by Hyperides. The great orator won the case by presenting the courtesan to the jury naked.

t par espriuient leprouuent

t qut tu auras same prise

u le sauras bien aduise

omment helouys labelle

traydit pieires abaelart

ieurs abaelart le confesse

Qui fu ct helouys labelle

u prandit qui fu samne

Heloise

◇◇◇

The letters of Heloise and Abelard are known to posterity as one of the most ancient testimonies of romantic, passionate love. Following a childhood spent in the nunnery at Argenteuil, Heloise is sent to Paris under the tutelage of her uncle, Canon Fulbert. The beauty and intelligence of the girl is soon the talk of the town. Attracted by the girl's reputation, the theologian Pierre Abélard, one of the most eminent teachers of the age, arranges to assist her with her studies, taking a room with the canon with the intention of seducing her.

They begin a relationship but it cannot be hidden long: Heloise becomes pregnant and gives birth to a son. To assuage Fulbert's anger, Heloise and Abelard wed, but, afraid of the effect on his career at the university, Abelard wants to keep the marriage secret. He has Heloise taken back into the convent at Argenteuil. Enraged, Fulbert has Abelard castrated, a punishment then reserved for adultery. This revenge, carried out in private in very heart of the chapterhouse of Notre-Dame on such a famous theologian, causes a scandal in the kingdom. Heloise takes the veil but continues a lifelong correspondence with her husband, eventually becoming abbess of the Abbey of the Paraclete. The romanticism of our story is tarnished somewhat because it seems the priory was ceded to the nuns by Abelard in the hope—vain as it turned out—of having it placed under his supervision. Despite their ordeals, Heloise always remained faithful to Abelard and they were buried side by side. In this delicate miniature, their story serves as a pretext for a scene of courtly love.

Ono no
Komachi

◇◇◇

In ninth-century Japan there lived a talented and attractive poetess who went by the name of Ono no Komachi. The only woman to be elected among the Six Immortal Poets, she became one of the great mythical figures of Japan. An aura surrounds this mysterious personality whose life was an inextricable blend of fantasy and reality.

According to stories at the time, Ono no Komachi was an exceptional beauty, admired and adored, and the cause of many passions. Probably married on several occasions, she had a string of liaisons. She loved and was loved, leaving a trail of devastation in her wake. Texts describe her as extravagant as she was proud, as irresistible as she was cruel.

"Men penned her billets-doux and love letters as innumerable as drops of rain falling from a summer sky. But answer sent she none, not a single word" (Sotoba Komachi). Her legend was embroidered with a stream of anecdotes. One tells of how she ordered one of her suitors, Captain Fukakusa, to play court to her for one hundred consecutive nights before allowing him to enter the chamber. The captain did as he was bidden for ninety-nine, but on the hundredth he failed to make an appearance: he had simply died of waiting.

But this much-admired woman had an unhappy end. Her twenty-one poems, all that survives of her oeuvre, are all tinged with poignant melancholy. After living in great pomp at the imperial court, her beauty faded and she sank into obscurity and then wretchedness. Abandoned by all, some accounts say that she died alone in a field. This print, typical of Hosoda Eishi's elegant style, shows Ono no Komachi, dressed in a splendid kimono billowing in the breeze, holding a piece of parchment, in a moment of inspiration. It captures well the passion and ardor of this captivating woman, whose allure was fatal to so many—and, in the end, even to herself.

Juliette Drouet, Charles-Émile-Callende de Champmartin, 1837,
oil on canvas, 23 ½ x 28 ¼ in. (60 x 72 cm), Musée Victor Hugo, Paris

Juliette
Drouet

◇◇

At her death, Juliette Drouet left thousands of letters written to the most important figure in her life and her lover for nearly fifty years: the poet, Victor Hugo. Finding herself motherless a few months after her birth and fatherless the following year, she was brought up by an uncle, René Drouet, before entering a Paris boarding school. Becoming the mistress of the sculptor James Pradier, by whom she had a daughter, Claire, she began, under his guidance, a career as an actress. This was how, in 1833, she met Victor Hugo, while performing the role of the princess Négroni in *Lucrèce Borgia*. Their first night of love, which fell on February 16/17 becomes—in *Les Misérables*—that of Marius and Cosette. Juliette gave up the theater to dedicate herself completely to her love. Throughout their lifetime, Hugo provided both for the needs of Juliette and her daughter.

One sees in this portrait a gentle yet determined individual. In spite of being betrayed—many times—by the great man, Juliette displayed unflinching constancy and fidelity in her relationship with Hugo. For many years, she lived, as the poet demanded, a sheltered existence in his house, leaving it solely in his company. At the same time Hugo's muse and intimate collaborator, Juliette possessed writing gifts of her own. Her letters reveal a character in which ardor is combined with extreme devotion. The woman who declared with passion to her "dear Victor," "I want you to kiss me to death, that's all," even saved the poet's life in December 1851, accompanying him on his exile to Brussels, then on to Jersey in 1852 and Guernsey in 1855.

Conforming to the image of the "eternal woman," Juliette Drouet was the compliant victim of a destiny entirely devoted to the man she adored. "The world has his thought. Me, I had his love," are the words inscribed on her tombstone.

L'Âge mûr (The Age of Maturity), **Camille Claudel**, c. 1902, bronze, 2 ft. 4 in. (72 cm) Musée d'Orsay, Paris

Camille
Claudel

◇◇

A reflection on both human life and the female condition, *The Age of Maturity* is also an artistic autobiography. The group, created after Camille Claudel broke up with Rodin, shows the sculptor hesitating, torn between his former mistress—who finally wins the day—and Camille, here depicted on her knees.

"The Implorer"—the name she bestowed on the figure she acts out here—springs forward, arms outstretched, trying in vain to hold on to the love of her life. Rodin, however, the personification of the Mature Man, flees Youth—represented by Camille—and is irresistibly drawn to Age, as illustrated by another woman with older features who pulls him towards her.

The whole group is permeated by a sense of headlong flight, an image of passing time and lost love. The poet Paul Claudel reacted to the work in the following words: "My sister Camille, so haughty, so proud, here imploring, humiliated, on her knees, and you know what is being ripped out of her in this very moment, before your very eyes—it's her soul."

Camille Claudel was not only a tragic figure in this sculpture; she was in life as well. With Camille, art and life overlapped to an extraordinary degree. Her ardent, passionate personality, expressed as much in her art as in her relationship with Rodin, meant that rejection could unsettle her mental health. Like her works, the liberated and original personality of this muse-cum-artist was considered provocative in a society where to be a woman sculptor was to challenge preconceptions. Critics were quick to insinuate that she owed everything to the "Great Man," just at the time she was striving to free herself from the sway and artistic influence that Rodin had over her. Fragile and sensitive, Camille eventually fell prey to paranoia.

Dora Maar

◇◇◇

O ne day, in the café Les Deux Magots, Picasso, in the company of his friend Paul Eluard, notices a beautiful young brunette seated at a nearby table. With a grave expression animated by bright and burning eyes, she is playing with a penknife that she sticks into the wooden table between her gloved fingers. Sometimes she misses her target and wounds herself. Picasso is fascinated. They leave the café together. At least that is the legend of their meeting.

Dora Maar was a flamboyant and intriguing personality, who wore recherché garb and eye-catching headgear and painted her nails in different colors depending on her mood. Her relationship with Picasso was one that combined love with artistic collaboration: lover, muse, and model, she was herself a photographer before becoming a painter.

Picasso often represented Dora in tears, saying that, "for me, Dora is a woman who weeps. For years, I painted her in tortured forms, not for sadism or pleasure. I did nothing but follow the vision imposed on me. That was the deep truth about Dora."

The woman who weeps, the essence of Dora Maar? Such an observation speaks volumes as to the tenuous border between empathy and projection that characterizes so many of Picasso's remarks. Shifting from the role of model to adopt that of painter, Dora produced a series of self-portraits that leant heavily on the theme of the *Dolorosa*, whose colors, backdrop, and atmosphere are modified so as to appropriate the image for herself. Their dramatic intensity is significantly less raw.

In summer, Dora and Picasso would often stay at Mougins in the company of Paul and Nusch Eluard, Lee Miller, Jacqueline Lamba, Man Ray, and others. The group would often swap partners and it is highly probable that Eluard's beautiful wife, a Surrealist muse of ethereal and fragile charm, had an affair with Picasso.

Dora and Picasso's passionate and stormy liaison lasted nearly nine years, though Picasso never broke off his relationship with Marie-Thérèse Walter. When he left Dora on meeting Françoise Gilot, she fell into a deep depression.

Frida
Kahlo

◇◇

Frida Kahlo produced this double self-portrait shortly after her divorce from the painter and printmaker Diego Rivera. On the right, dressed in Mexican costume, sits the Frida her husband loved, holding an amulet set with a miniature portrait of him.

On the left there's another Frida, the one Diego no longer loves, wearing a white lace-trimmed dress in a more Western style. This side of her looks as though she might be drained of blood. The stormy sky reflects a turbulent crisis in their marriage. As she was wont to do, Kahlo exposes the figures' hearts, metaphors of her inner turmoil.

In many respects, the present picture represents the antithesis of a wedding portrait executed in 1931. Diego and Frida appear side by side and hand in hand. *The Two Fridas* can be interpreted as an exploration of the role of woman in a couple. Frida in her wedding dress would represent the young wife and the bleeding flowers would allude to the defloration of the bride in traditional marriage, to her entrance into the married state. Blood, the torn dress, the broken artery, the heart sliced in two then illustrate the suffering she experienced during her marriage. The Frida on the right-hand side stands for woman as she becomes a mother.

The egg-shaped portrait form of Diego as a child that she holds in front of her uterus might be an allusion to the "little Diego" whom Frida so wanted to bring into the world. But, victim of an almost fatal accident, she could never have safely given birth. Portrayed on one side as a woman without a man and on the other as a mother without a child, Frida Kahlo here expresses her inability to conform to the conventions of female identity of her age.

But the image can also be interpreted differently: some time after their initial breakup, Diego and Frida got back together and remarried. Their relationship, though, had changed significantly. Frida now understood that, if she wanted to stay with Diego, the only viable option was to become *his* mother—just as in the painting, where the portrait of the child Diego is placed on her womb.

The Two Fridas, **Frida Kahlo,** 1939,
oil on canvas, 67 x 67 in. (170 x 170 cm), Museo de Arte Moderno, Mexico City

Rita Hayworth in *Gilda*, **a film by Charles Vidor,** 1946

Rita
Hayworth

The love life of the woman nicknamed the "Goddess of Love" was in fact tragic. "All I wanted was just what everyone else wants, you know, to be loved." Her stormy existence amounted to one long search for the happiness and affection that she never found. Femme fatale on the silver screen, as here in *Gilda,* where she has a string of affairs and arouses the uncontrollable jealousy of a former lover (Glenn Ford), in real life she tended to be the one who suffered.

Throughout her life and career, Rita Hayworth was manipulated by men, some of whom were near psychopaths. The first was her father, a dancer of Spanish extraction, who, absolutely determined to turn her into an accomplished exponent of his art, worked her to a standstill. He would perform with his daughter onstage, forming a couple that advanced his career; in private, he had incestuous relations with her on a daily basis.

This tragic experience was probably at the root of her disastrous love life. Over and again, the same painful script was played out: her first husband, Eddie Judson, suggested she share the beds of potential producers. When the infatuated Harry Cohn, President of Columbia Pictures, demanded she change her style of clothing and undergo plastic surgery, Rita did as she was told. But when she rejected his advances, he found myriad ways of humiliating her.

Her marriage with Orson Welles was no less of a fiasco. The actor-director had fallen head over heels in love with Rita on seeing a photograph, and was intent on marrying her even though they'd never met. But Rita was no Gilda.... Prince Ali Khan, her third husband, having led her up the garden path, embarked on a string of adulterous affairs. Her next husband, the singer Dick Haymes, an alcoholic, resorted to physical violence. The fifth, the producer James Hill, in spite of his promise to steer her away from the studio, in fact exploited her and forced her to shoot film after film until she was exhausted. He seemed, she remarked, to treat her as a business. In more than one respect, Rita Hayworth's life is a prime example of the cruel way Hollywood treats its stars.

Marilyn
Monroe

◇◇◇

The epitome of sex appeal, Marilyn Monroe became a victim of her own extraordinary charm. Her marriage with the popular baseball player Joe DiMaggio lasted only eight months, while the one to the playwright Arthur Miller also ended in divorce. A serious bout of depression forced her to leave the shoot of her last film, *Something's Got to Give* (1962), and it remained unfinished. The mystery surrounding her tragic death completes the myth of Marilyn.

The characters she played onscreen were ultimately never that dangerous. If in *Niagara* (1953) she stars as a perverse femme fatale who manipulates a man to make him kill her husband, on the whole Marilyn embodied, in a light and bubbly spirit, the irresistible and often "dumb" blonde, as in *Gentlemen Prefer Blondes* (1953), in which she takes the part of a gold-digger, *How to Marry a Millionaire* (1953), *The Seven-year Itch* (1955), and *Some Like It Hot* (1959).

Yet, above and beyond the films she featured in, it is her personality that remains engraved on the collective memory. Her image is tangible in *Blonde,* a recent novel by Joyce Carol Oates, broadly inspired by Marilyn's life, in which the author presents her as a figure of femininity exploited by men and destroyed by the desire she arouses. Much like Rita Hayworth (see p.153) and others too, she is indicative of the kind of curse that affects women who are promoted as sex symbols.

Credits

Bibliography for Laure Adler's text

Agacinski, Sylviane, *Drame des sexes*, Paris: Seuil, 2008.

Arasse, Daniel, *Le Détail, pour une histoire rapprochée de la peinture*, Paris: Flammarion, 2008.

Bard, Christine, *Les Filles de Marianne*, Paris: Fayard, 1995.

Bartolena, Simona, and Ida Giordano, *Femmes artistes de la Renaissance au XXIᵉ siècle*, Paris: Gallimard, 2003.

Bernadac, Marie-Laure, and Bernard Marcadé, *Féminin-masculin, le sexe de l'art*, Paris: Éditions du Centre Georges Pompidou/Gallimard, 1995.

Bonnet, Marie-Jo, *Les Femmes dans l'art*, Paris: Éditions de La Martinière, 2004.

Bourgeois, Louise, and Marie-Laure Bernadac, *Louise Bourgeois*, Paris: Flammarion, 2006.

Butler, Judith, *Undoing Gender*, London: Routledge, 2004.

Calle, Sophie, *Prenez soin de vous*, Arles: Actes sud, 2007.

Chastel, André, *French Art. Renaissance,* vol. 2, Paris: Flammarion, 2000.

Chastel, André, *French Art. Ancien Régime 1620-1775*, vol. 3, Paris: Flammarion, 2000.

Collective, *Femmes-femmes, Regard de femmes, Femmes regardées*, Arles: Actes sud, 2002.

Des Cars, Laurence, *Gustave Courbet, l'œuvre de Courbet et sa logique en image*, Paris: RMN, 2007.

Epron, Nathalie, *Création, où sont les femmes?* Montbonnot-Saint-Martin: Terres d'éclat, 2004.

Fraisse, Geneviève, *Du consentement*, Paris: Seuil, 2007.

Gonnard, Catherine, and Élisabeth Lebovici, *Femmes artistes/artistes femmes: Paris, de 1880 à nos jours*, Paris: Hazan, 2007.

Grenier, Catherine, *Annette Messager* (tr. D. Radzinowicz), Paris: Flammarion, 2001.

Heller, Nancy G., *Women Artists. An Illustrated History*, New York: Abbeville, 2004.

Héritier, Françoise, *Masculin/Féminin, la pensée de la différence*, vol. 1, Paris: Odile Jacob, 1996.

Héritier, Françoise, *Masculin/Féminin, dissoudre la hiérarchie*, vol. 2, Paris: Odile Jacob, 2002.

Kristeva, Julia, *Thérèse mon amour: sainte Thérèse d'Ávila*, Paris: Fayard, 2008.

Michelet, Jules, *Satanism and Witchcraft: A Study in Medieval Superstition* (trans. A. R. Allinson), London: Lyle Stuart/Citadel Press, 1939 [1862].

Millet, Catherine, *The Sexual Life of Catherine M.* (tr. A. Hunter), London: Serpent's Tail, 2002.

Murat, Laure, *La Loi du genre: une histoire culturelle du troisième sexe*, Paris: Fayard, 2006.

Perrot, Michelle, and Georges Duby, *History of Women in the West. Nineteenth Century* (trans. A. Goldhammer et. al.), vol. 4, Cambridge, MA: Harvard University Press, Belknap Press, 1994.

Perrot, Michelle, *Mon histoire des femmes*, Paris: Seuil ("Points histoire"), 2008.

Picq, Françoise, *Libération des femmes: les années mouvement*, Paris: Seuil, 1993.

Sacchi, Henri, and Geneviève Fraisse, *L'Exercice du savoir et la différence des sexes*, Paris: L'Harmattan, 2000.

Stevens Prioleau, Elizabeth, *Seductress. Women Who Ravished the World and Their Lost Art of Love*, London: Penguin Books, 2004.

Woolf, Virginia, *A Room of One's Own*, London: Penguin Books, 2002 [1921].

Cinderella's Sisters Preparing for the Ball, **William Wegman**, 1992, photograph 20 x 24 in. (61 x 80.8 cm), Shaheen Modern & Contemporary Art, Cleveland